OXFORD

COMBINED STUDENT'S BOOK & WORKBOOK

Paul A Davies & Tim Falla

FLASHLIGHT CONTENTS

Reading	Everyday English and Listening	Writing
	• Introducing people	
• Football dreams	• Making arrangements (present continuous for future arrangements) • Rachel and Dan make arrangements	• A personal description • Expressing contrast: *but*, *although*, *however*, *on the other hand*
• Liverpool – city of change	• Expressing likes and dislikes • Similar or different tastes in music?	• My town, then and now • Structuring an essay
• Synaesthesia	• At the doctor's • An accident	• Personal memories • Brainstorming
• Splitting up is hard to do	• At a restaurant • Complaining in a restaurant	• History of a relationship • *both … and …*, *neither … nor*
• Sixteen and serious	• At the post office • Sending letters and getting a new passport	• A formal letter • Job application letter

Introduction

UNIT FOCUS
- Vocabulary revision
- Present simple
- Present continuous
- Past simple
- Question words
- Introducing people

DAN'S STORY Opposites attract

1 They say that opposites attract. That's true for me and my girlfriend, Rachel. Our personalities are completely different, but we love spending time together. Rachel is quiet, sensitive and artistic. She worries about things – exams, relationships, the future. I hardly every worry. What's the point? My attitude is: enjoy life, and don't look for complications.

It's really sunny. Put down that book and let's go outside.

I can't. I'm revising for an exam. Ask Hanif.

2 Hanif is my best friend. We went to the same primary school, and now we're in the same class at secondary school. We've got similar interests too. We both like music, road bikes … and girls. Hanif has usually got his eye on one of Rachel's friends, and she's got a new friend – Abby. It's Abby's first week at our school, and Rachel is looking after her.

4 That's another thing about me – I sometimes open my mouth without thinking. I'm not insensitive. It's just honesty … isn't it?

1 Read and listen to Dan's story. True or false? Correct the false sentences.

1 Rachel is Dan's boyfriend.
2 Rachel is Hanif's best friend.
3 Abby is a new girl at Dan's school.

2 Write the correct names.

1 ...... is quiet, sensitive and artistic.
2 ...... hardly ever worries.
3 ...... is interested in Rachel's friends.
4 ...... is Rachel's new friend.

3 Answer the questions.

1 What does Rachel worry about?
2 What are Dan and Hanif interested in?
3 When Hanif says 'She's gorgeous', is he talking about Abby's appearance or her personality?
4 Why is Rachel annoyed with Dan?

4 **REAL ENGLISH** Find equivalents for these sentences in the story.

1 What reason is there to do it?
2 Hanif is usually interested in one of Rachel's friends.
3 Well done.
4 I sometimes speak without thinking.

5 **REAL ENGLISH** Rewrite the underlined words with expressions from exercise 4.

1 I don't buy CDs. What reason is there to do it when you can download music?
2 I haven't got a boyfriend, but I'm interested in my brother's friend.
3 'I passed my exam!' 'Well done!'
4 She often comes out with us, but she never speaks.

What do you think?

Do you agree or disagree?

- Dan's attitude to life is good.
- Dan isn't insensitive. He's just honest.
- I like people who are very different from me.

Vote YES or NO for each one and give your reasons.

Vocabulary

Revision

6 Find examples of these words in the story.

1 a phrasal verb (in the first photo)
2 five personality adjectives
3 two interests

7 Match the words in the box with the correct groups in the chart.

collecting things fashion funny generous magazines moody pick up take off turn on

Phrasal verbs	Personality adjectives	Interests

8 Complete the sentences. Use words from exercise 7.

1 He's not very .... He never gives anybody anything.
2 You should ...... your dirty shoes before you go inside.
3 I always read the cookery sections of ...... first.
4 Can you ...... the light, please?
5 John loves .... He's always buying clothes.
6 Kate's a bit ...... – sometimes she's friendly, but sometimes she doesn't even say hello.
7 Your room is untidy. Can you ...... your clothes from the floor?
8 Dave's very ...... – he's always telling jokes.
9 My Dad loves .... He's got stamps, coins and lots of postcards..

9 Write descriptions of yourself and one of your friends. Write about personality and interests.

I'm going to describe me and ...
Our personalities are similar/different.
My friend ... is very ... and ... . I'm ...
We've got similar/different interests.
I like ...
He/She's interested in ...

More practice? Workbook page 68

GRAMMAR 1

Present simple

1 Study the sentences. Do you remember the forms and the spelling rules ?

> Rachel **worries** a lot.
> Dan and Rachel **don't have** lessons together.
> 'Does Hanif **like** Abby?' 'Yes, he **does**.'

2 Complete the text with the verbs in the box. Use the present simple, affirmative or negative.

> go live not ask not go
> not want study use worry

Hi, my name's Hanif. I'm 17 and I (**1**) ...... in London. I (**2**) ...... to Greenfield Secondary School.

My sister, Fatima, is 18 and she (**3**) ...... languages at East London College. Dad (**4**) ...... about her a lot, because he (**5**) ...... her to fail her exams.

My brother, Zaman, is only nine so he (**6**) ...... to my school. He's at Greenfield Primary School. He's really annoying. He (**7**) ...... my computer when I'm out but he (**8**) ...... me first. And he's always in the shower when I want to use the bathroom.

3 Complete the questions about Hanif.

'Where *does he live*?' 'In London.'

1. 'Which school ...... ?' 'Greenfield Secondary School.'
2. 'What ...... Hanif and Dan ...... ?' 'Road bikes.'
3. 'What ...... Fatima ...... ?' 'Languages.'
4. 'Why ...... their dad ...... about Fatima?' 'Because he doesn't want her to fail her exams.'
5. 'When ...... Zaman ...... Hanif's computer?' 'When he's out.'

More practice? Workbook pages 69–70

Present continuous

4 Study the sentences. Do you remember the spelling rules for *-ing* forms?

> I'**m revising** for an exam.
> He **isn't revising** for an exam.
> '**Are** you **revising** for an exam?' 'Yes, I **am**.'

5 Complete the rule

subject + correct form of the verb ...... + the ...... form

6 Look at the photo. Write sentences about Abby and Rachel. Use the present continuous, affirmative and negative.

chat *Abby and Rachel are chatting.*

1. drink / tea
2. not sit / floor
3. look at / photos
4. not wear / jeans
5. wear / a green top

7 Put the words in the correct order to make questions in the present continuous. Then answer them.

your / is / talking / teacher
Is your teacher talking?
No, he/she isn't.

1. wearing / you / jeans / are
2. is / smiling / teacher / your
3. mum / are / working / and dad / your
4. raining / is / it
5. you / sitting / are / next to / your best friend
6. studying / are / friends / your

More practice? Workbook pages 69–70

Dialogue

1 Read and listen. What is happening?

a) Hanif is introducing Rachel to Abby.
b) Rachel is introducing Abby to Hanif.
c) Abby is introducing Rachel to Hanif.

Introducing people

Rachel	Hanif, this is Abby. She's new.
Hanif	Hi, Abby.
Abby	Hi, Hanif. Nice to meet you.
Hanif	And you.
Rachel	Abby's from Liverpool.
Abby	We moved here last month.
Hanif	How come?
Abby	My dad got a new job in London.
Hanif	Oh right. Do you miss home?
Abby	Yes, I do. I really miss my friends.
Hanif	Well, if you fancy going out at the weekend, give me a call.
Abby	Thanks!

2 REAL ENGLISH Listen and repeat these expressions. What do they mean?

1 How come?
2 Do you miss …?
3 … , if you fancy going out …
4 … give me a call.

3 Practise reading the dialogue.

4 Write your own dialogue. Use ideas from the box or invent your own.

We moved because:
my mum got a new job.
most of my family live near here.
I really miss:
the sea / the countryside / the mountains.
my old school.

A: … , this is … . He/She's new.
B: Hi, …
C: Hi, … Nice to meet you.

5 Act out your dialogue.

More practice? Workbook page 70

Listening

6 Listen to Rachel and Abby. What do they arrange?

a) To meet at the café and then see a film at the cinema.
b) To meet at the cinema and go to the café after the film.

7 Listen again. Are the sentences true or false? Correct the false ones.

1 Abby's first week at school was OK.
2 Rachel usually goes out with her friends on Saturday.
3 Abby suggests that she meets Rachel on Sunday.
4 Abby likes martial arts films, but she doesn't like adventure films.
5 They arrange to meet in the café at five o'clock.
6 The café is near the school.

GRAMMAR 2

Past simple

1 Are these verbs regular or irregular?

be chat eat feel give go like meet phone sit stop study walk worry

2 Write the past simple forms of the verbs in exercise 1. Check the Irregular verbs list on page 56.

3 How do we form the negative and interrogative? Complete the table.

Negative
She (**1**) …… to the cinema. (not go) She (**2**) …… the film. (not see)
Interrogative
(**3**) …… she …… to the cinema? (go) (**4**) …… she …… the film? (see)

4 Complete the email. Use the past simple affirmative, negative or interrogative.

Hi Grace!
(**1** you / get) my text message? I (**2** send) it from school on my first morning. I (**3** not be) very happy then! I (**4** not like) anything or anybody! But things (**5** get) better later that day. I (**6** meet) a really nice girl called Rachel, and we (**7** chat) for ages. We (**8** go) out together last weekend. What (**9** you and Mark / do) last weekend? (**10** you / go out)?
Abby
xx

More practice? Workbook pages 69–70

Question words

5 Complete the rules. Use the question words in the box.

how how many how much how often ~~what~~ when where which who whose why

1 We use what and …… to ask about things.
2 We use …… to ask about people.
3 We use …… to ask about possession.
4 We use …… to ask about time.
5 We use …… to ask about place.
6 We use …… to ask for a reason.
7 We use …… to ask about manner or method.
8 We use …… to ask about frequency.
9 We use …… to ask about quantity.
10 We use …… to ask about number.

6 Complete the questions with words from exercise 5. Then ask and answer in pairs.

1 …… did you do last night?
2 …… do you go to bed after midnight?
3 …… do you live?
4 …… did you travel to school this morning?
5 …… brothers and sisters have you got?
6 …… do you prefer, rice or pasta?
7 …… is your favourite film star?
8 …… homework do you usually do at weekends?

What did you do last night?

I played computer games.

More practice? Workbook pages 69–70

Communicate!

Write five questions about what your partner did last weekend. Use five question words. Then ask and answer in pairs.
Where did you go on Friday evening?

Learning Diary page 71

1 The right image

UNIT FOCUS

- Describing appearance
- *-ed* and *-ing* adjectives
- Present tense contrast
- *like*/*hate*, etc. + gerund
- Subject and object questions
- Making arrangements (present continuous for future arrangements)
- Expressing contrast: *but*, *although*, *however*, *on the other hand*

VOCABULARY

Describing appearance

1 Match the words in the box with the pictures (1–10). Then listen and check.

bracelet dyed hair earring glasses make-up necklace piercings ring sunglasses tattoo

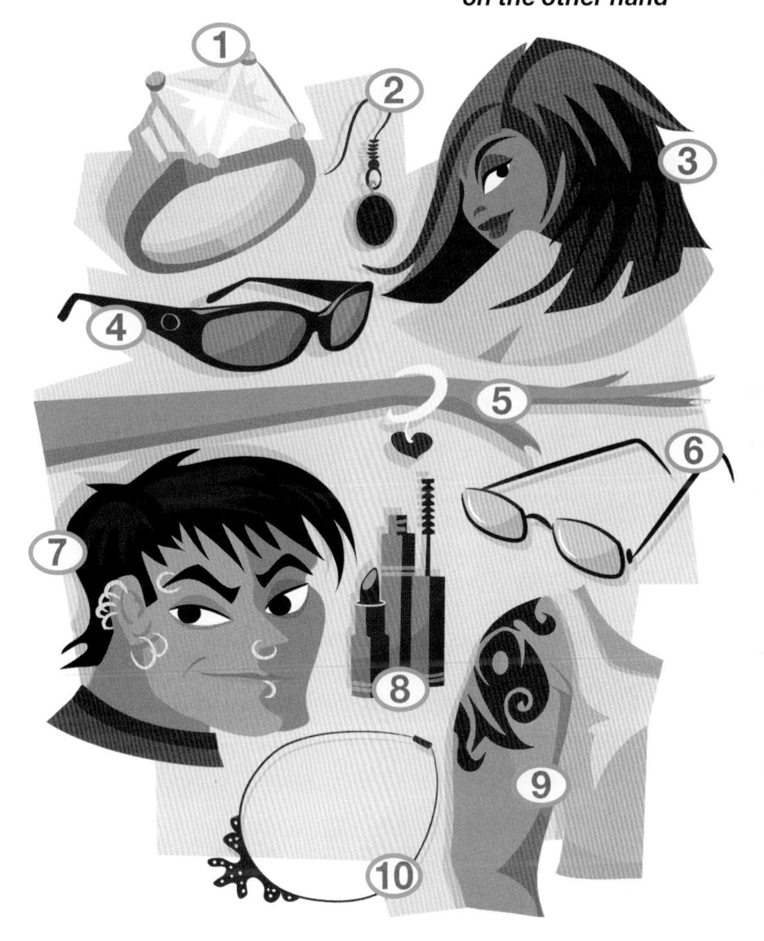

Take note!

We use *wear* with things you put on and take off:
He's wearing a ring. She's wearing make-up.
We use *have got* with items you don't put on or take off:
He's got a tattoo. She's got dyed hair.

2 Write six sentences about you, your friends and your family.

My sister doesn't wear any make-up, but she's got a tattoo on her arm.

3 Listen and repeat the words in the box. What do they mean?

casual old-fashioned scruffy smart sporty trendy

4 Look at the pictures and listen. Which person is being described?

5 Describe the other five people in the pictures. Use words from exercises 1 and 3.

She/He looks ...
She's/He's got ...
She's/He's wearing ...

More practice? Workbook page 72

a

b

c

d

e

f

RACHEL'S STORY You can't wear that!

1 There's a market every Sunday in London called Spitalfields market. I often go there to look for clothes and CDs. Today, I'm taking Abby there for the first time. Dan and Hanif are coming along too. Hanif likes shopping for clothes, but Dan isn't really into fashion. He prefers buying CDs.

2 Hanif wears trendy clothes. Bright colours really suit him because of his black hair and dark skin. He often wears hats too. Dan looks good in a pair of jeans and a T-shirt, but he doesn't wear bright colours – and hats look ridiculous. I don't know why, but they really don't suit him.

3 It was only a joke, but Dan didn't take it very well. He looked hurt for a moment, and that's unusual for him – he's usually really cheerful. I tried to explain, but I made it worse. Help! Why are relationships so difficult?

1 Read and listen to Rachel's story. Why does Dan get upset?

2 Answer the questions.

1 What do Rachel, Hanif and Dan each like shopping for?
2 What suits Hanif?
3 What clothes suit Dan?
4 According to Rachel, what doesn't suit Dan?
5 Does Rachel offend Dan on purpose?
6 Why is Rachel surprised when Dan gets upset?
7 What happens when Rachel tries to explain?

3 True or false? Correct the false sentences.

1 The market is open every day.
2 It's Abby's first time at the market.
3 Hanif often wears hats.
4 Rachel thinks relationships are easy.

4 **REAL ENGLISH** Find equivalents for these sentences in the story.

1 Dan and Hanif are coming with us.
2 Dan isn't really interested in fashion.
3 He looked upset.
4 That hat doesn't suit you.

5 **REAL ENGLISH** Rewrite the underlined words with expressions from exercise 4.

1 Carol and I went to a football match yesterday. Carol's boyfriend came with us.
2 I'm not really interested in computers.
3 She was upset because I forgot her birthday.
4 Baseball caps don't suit me.

What do you think?

Do you agree or disagree with these statements?
- Dan is wrong to feel hurt.
- Rachel is wrong to make a joke about Dan's appearance.
- Trendy clothes don't suit everybody.

Vote YES or NO for each one and give your reasons.

Word help

-ed and *-ing* adjectives

6 Copy and complete the chart.

If a person or thing is …	boring annoying (2) …… exciting (4) …… surprising (6) …… disappointing (8) ……	then you are …	bored. (1) …… . embarrassed. (3) …… . interested. (5) …… . confused. (7) …… . frightened.

7 Choose the correct adjectives.

1 I'm really **annoying/annoyed** because I can't find my mobile phone.
2 England won the World Cup. I'm **surprising/surprised**.
3 I don't like this film. It's **boring/bored**.
4 I forgot her name. It was really **embarrassing/embarrassed**.
5 I love parties. They're really **exciting/excited**.
6 This TV programme is very **interesting/interested**.

More practice? Workbook page 72

Pronunciation Word stress and syllables

1 Listen and repeat the words. Have they got two syllables or three syllables?

boring embarrassed excited
gorgeous interesting surprised

boring – two syllables

2 Listen again and mark the stress. Is it on the first or second syllable?

bóring (first syllable)

GRAMMAR 1

Present tense contrast

1 **Study the sentences and match the sentences (1–4) with the uses (a–d).**

Present simple
1 Hanif often **wears** hats. 2 Rachel **lives** in London.
Present continuous
3 Look! Dan **is wearing** a hat! 4 Rachel's cousin **is living** in Manchester while she's at university.

a) a fact or a permanent situation
b) a temporary situation
c) an action that happens regularly or always
d) an action that's happening now

Watch out!

Some verbs are not usually used in the present continuous.

believe hate know like love need prefer remember taste understand want

~~Are you knowing Ben?~~ ✗
Do you know Ben? ✓

2 **Choose the correct verb forms.**

1 He ...... smart when he goes out.
a) always looks **b)** 's always looking
2 Dolphins ...... fish.
a) eat **b)** are eating
3 She ...... make-up today.
a) wears **b)** 's wearing
4 I ...... in a hotel for the next two weeks.
a) stay **b)** 'm staying
5 I ...... what you're thinking!
a) know **b)** 'm knowing
6 We can't go out. It ....
a) rains **b)** 's raining

3 **Complete the sentences. Use the present simple or present continuous.**

1 Look. That boy ...... (wear) a pair of Diesel jeans.
2 'Where's Mary?' 'She ...... (play) volleyball. She always ...... (go) to the sports centre on Friday evening.'
3 I ......(not want) these chips. They ......(taste) awful.
4 '...... (you have) a nice time?' 'Yes, thanks.'
5 'What's that awful noise?'
'It's my sister. She ...... (sing).'
6 '...... (you / know) where John is?'
'In his bedroom. He ...... (do) his homework.'

4 **Complete the conversation. Use the present simple or present continuous. Then listen and check.**

Millie What (**1** you / do)?
Karen I (**2** read) my horoscope.
Millie (**3** you / believe) in horoscopes?
Karen Yes. It says here, 'At the moment you (**4** try) to change your image.' That's true! I (**5** want) to look more trendy.
Millie Oh really … I'm bored. (**6** you / want) to go out?
Karen OK. Let's go and see Steve.
Millie He (**7** play) football now. He always (**8** play) football on Saturday mornings.
Karen Well, in that case I (**9** go) to the shops to buy some clothes. (**10** you / come)?
Millie No, thanks. I think I'll stay here.

More practice? **Workbook pages 73–74**

Dialogue

1 Read and listen. Complete the dialogue with the words in the box.

hello like moment tomorrow way

Making arrangements

Abby's mum	457 3342. Hello?
Hanif	Oh, (**1**) .... Can I speak to Abby, please?
Abby's mum	Yes. Who's calling?
Hanif	Hanif.
Abby's mum	Just a (**2**) ...... , please.
Abby	Hi, Hanif. How are you?
Hanif	Fine. What are you doing (**3**) ......?
Abby	Nothing special. Why?
Hanif	I'm watching a DVD at Dan's house. Would you (**4**) ...... to come?
Abby	Um, yes. Is Rachel going too?
Hanif	Yes, of course.
Abby	What time are you going?
Hanif	At about five o'clock. I'll call for you on the (**5**) ...... , if you like.
Abby	OK, thanks.

2 **REAL ENGLISH** Listen and repeat these expressions. What do they mean?

1 Can I speak to Abby, please?
2 Who's calling?
3 Nothing special.
4 I'll call for you.

3 Practise reading the dialogue.

4 Write your own dialogue. Use ideas from the box or invent your own.

listen to CDs play computer games
watch a football match
watch a film on TV

A: (telephone number). Hello?
B: Oh, hello. Can I speak to ... , please?

5 Act out your dialogue.

More practice? Workbook page 74

Listening

6 Listen to Rachel and Dan. What do they arrange to do this evening?

a) watch a film at Dan's house
b) go to the cinema
c) go out for something to eat
d) go to a disco

7 Listen again. Answer the questions.

1 What does Rachel want to apologise for?
2 Is Dan still feeling upset?
3 Where is the present from?
4 What kind of film is the new Brad Pitt film?
5 How many people are going to watch the film tomorrow evening at Dan's house?
6 Does Dan wear his new T-shirt to go out?

like/hate, etc. + gerund

Take note!

A gerund is the *-ing* form of a verb, but it's a noun. We can use gerunds after verbs that express likes and dislikes, e.g. *like*, *love*, *hate*, *prefer*, *don't mind*, *enjoy*.
I don't mind **cooking**, but I prefer **washing** the dishes.

1 Complete the sentences. Use the gerund form of the verbs in the box.

buy dance get up go listen play shop walk watch

1 I hate ...... early.
2 'Do you like football?' 'I like ...... it on TV, but I don't like ...... it.'
3 He likes discos because he enjoys ....
4 I don't mind ...... to school, but I prefer ...... by bike.
5 She hates ...... for clothes, but she likes ...... magazines and books.
6 I love ...... to music when I study.

2 Work in pairs. Ask about the items in box A. Choose answers from box B.

A dance write letters travel by bus shop for clothes sing get up early

B Yes, I love it. I don't mind it. No, I don't like it. No, I hate it.

Do you like dancing?

No, I hate it. What about you? Do you like dancing?

Communicate!

Write five sentences about your friends and family. Use *like*, *love*, *hate*, *enjoy* etc. + gerund.
My dad enjoys eating fish.

More practice? Workbook pages 73–74

Subject and object questions

Take note!

When *who* or *what* is the object of a question, we use the auxiliary *do*.
What **does** he want?
(*What* = object, *he* = subject)
Who **did** you see at the party?
(*Who* = object, *you* = subject)
When *who* or *what* is the subject of a question, we don't use the auxiliary *do*.
What happened? **(*What* = subject)**
Who saw the film? **(*Who* = subject, *the film* = object)**

3 Write questions with *who* or *what*.

1 '(who / score) the second goal?' 'Zidane.'
2 '(what / you / do)?' 'I'm a student.'
3 '(who / you / sit) next to in class?' 'I sit next to Juan.'
4 '(who / phone) yesterday?' 'Gemma.'
5 '(what / you / have) for breakfast?' 'Toast'.

4 Write subject or object questions to ask about the missing information (???).

(???) won the World Cup in 2002.
Who won the World Cup in 2002?
Sony invented (???) in 1978.
What did Sony invent in 1978?

1 (???) starred in the film *Gladiator*?
2 Columbus brought back (???) from America.
3 (???) married Jennifer Lopez in 2004.
4 Polar bears eat (???).
5 (???) freezes at –210° Celsius.
6 A NASA spacecraft found (???) on Mars.

5 Now ask and answer the questions in exercise 4. Choose answers from the box.

Brazil fish and seals ice nitrogen Marc Anthony the CD tobacco Russell Crowe

More practice? Workbook pages 73–74

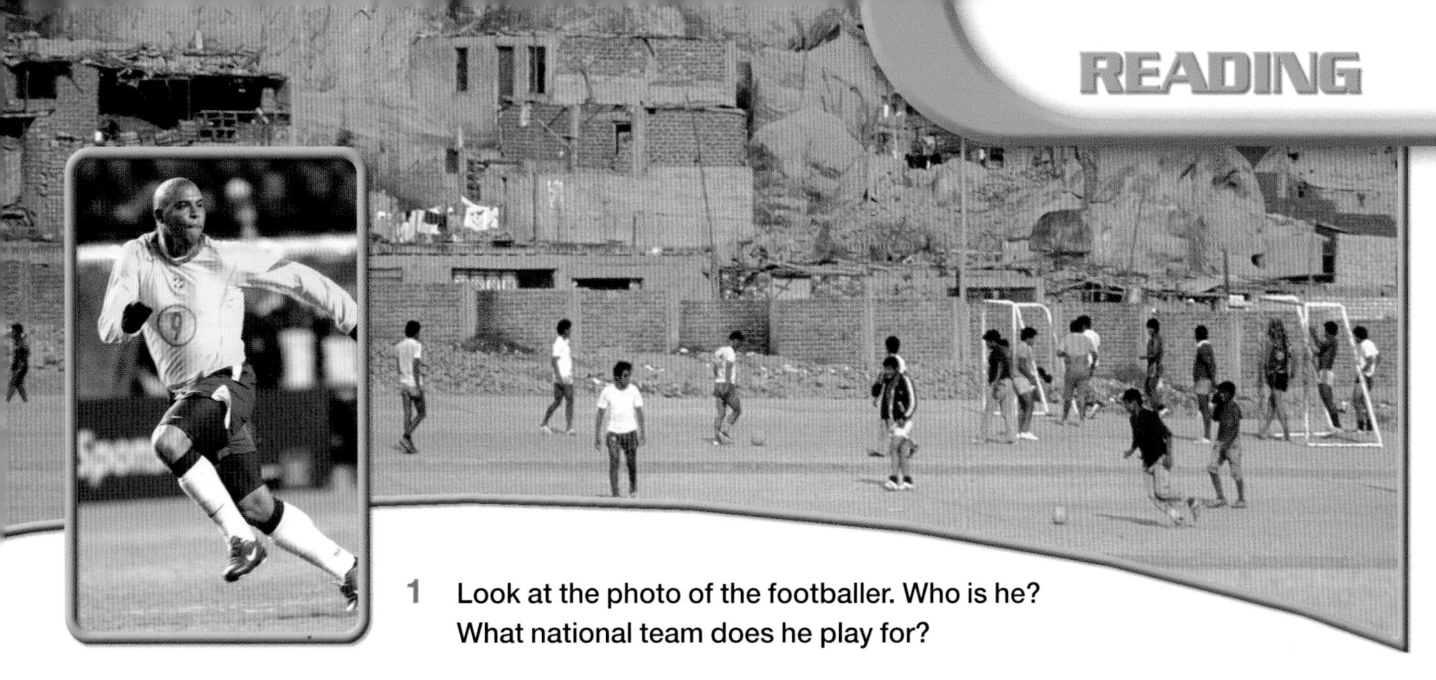

1 Look at the photo of the footballer. Who is he? What national team does he play for?

2 Read the text. Why is football so important to boys in the shanty towns?

Football dreams

Football isn't a hobby in Brazil – it's an obsession. Brazilians love watching, playing and talking about it. But for millions of Brazilian boys, there's another reason why football is so important.

[5] There are huge shanty towns in Rio de Janeiro and São Paulo. Life is very hard for the inhabitants. There aren't any proper houses, so families live in small shelters, often without water or electricity. Many children don't go to school, and without [10] education, it's very difficult to escape these terrible conditions. Football is their best chance of a new life, so they play for hours every day in the streets. They become very skilful players. And they all have the same dream – to play for Brazil and become [15] famous.

Of course, most of the boys don't succeed, but a few are lucky. One example is Ronaldo. He's from a shanty town in Rio. Does he ever think about the shanty towns now? The answer is yes. Ronaldo is [20] helping with a new project in one of the shanty towns of Rio, Ciudad de Dios. The project is the idea of MV Bill, a Brazilian rap artist. They're building a new community centre, with a cinema, a theatre and a museum. Life is getting better for [25] the 100,000 inhabitants of Ciudad de Dios, but for most of the boys there, football is still their dream.

3 Answer the questions.

1 What do Brazilians think of football?
2 What are conditions like in the shanty towns?
3 How long do boys in the shanty towns spend playing football?
4 What do these boys hope to do in the future?
5 Which two famous people are helping with a project in Ciudad de Dios?
6 How many people live in Ciudad de Dios?

4 **WORD CHECK** Find the words (1–5) in the text. Then match them with the meanings (a–e).

1 shanty towns (line 5)
2 shelters (line 8)
3 skilful (line 13)
4 community centre (line 23)
5 inhabitants (line 25)

a) good at doing something difficult
b) people who live in a place
c) towns with a lot of people but without proper buildings
d) places where you are safe from bad weather
e) a place where people in a town can meet and do activities

WRITING

Model text A personal description

1 Read the text. Find these words and phrases: *but*, *although*, *however*, *on the other hand*.

My image
I don't think I'm particularly trendy. I usually wear jeans and a top, or a tracksuit. However, I sometimes wear smart clothes on special occasions, like New Year. I never wear make-up, but I sometimes wear jewellery.

Three things that I love
I really like waking up on Saturday and knowing that I don't have to go to school. It's a great feeling, although I don't mind school when I'm there. I also love going out with a big group of friends to a café or to the cinema. The third thing I love is my new mobile! I can take photos with it and send them to my friends. However, only two friends can receive them.

Three things that I hate
I don't like intolerant people who never listen to other people's opinions. The second thing I hate is having arguments with my friends. It really upsets me, although fortunately we don't have arguments very often. The third thing I hate is sports programmes on television. My dad and brothers, on the other hand, always watch them, and they hardly ever let me watch programmes that I like!

2 True or false? Correct the false sentences.

1. Carol is very trendy.
2. She doesn't always wear jewellery.
3. She really hates school.
4. She can take photos with her new mobile.
5. She doesn't like intolerant people.
6. She often has arguments with her friends.

Expressing contrast

Take note!

We use *but* and *although* to express contrast within a sentence. We put a comma before them.
It's a great feeling, **although** I don't mind school when I'm there.
We use *however* and *on the other hand* to express contrast between sentences. We put a comma after them.
I can send photos to my friends. **However,** only two friends can receive them.

3 Choose the correct words and phrases. Add the commas.

1. I love jewellery **but** / **on the other hand** I don't like tattoos.
2. He looks scruffy. **But** / **However** he looks quite cool.
3. I can't stand mobile phones **although** / **however** they're quite useful
4. She's a bit moody. **Although** / **On the other hand** she's very generous.
5. I hate travelling by plane **on the other hand** / **although** it's the quickest form of transport.

Writing task

4 Write a text about yourself. Use the writing guide to help you.

Paragraph 1: My image
I think / don't think I'm ...
I usually wear ...
However, I sometimes wear ...
Paragraph 2: Three things that I love
I really like ... I also love ...
The third thing ...
Paragraph 3: Three things that I hate
I don't like ... The second thing ...
The third thing ...

More practice? Workbook page 75

Learning Diary page 76

2 Changes

UNIT FOCUS

- The urban landscape
- Extreme adjectives
- Past simple and past continuous
- *used to*
- Expressing likes and dislikes
- Structuring an essay

VOCABULARY

The urban landscape

1 Listen and repeat the words. What do they mean?

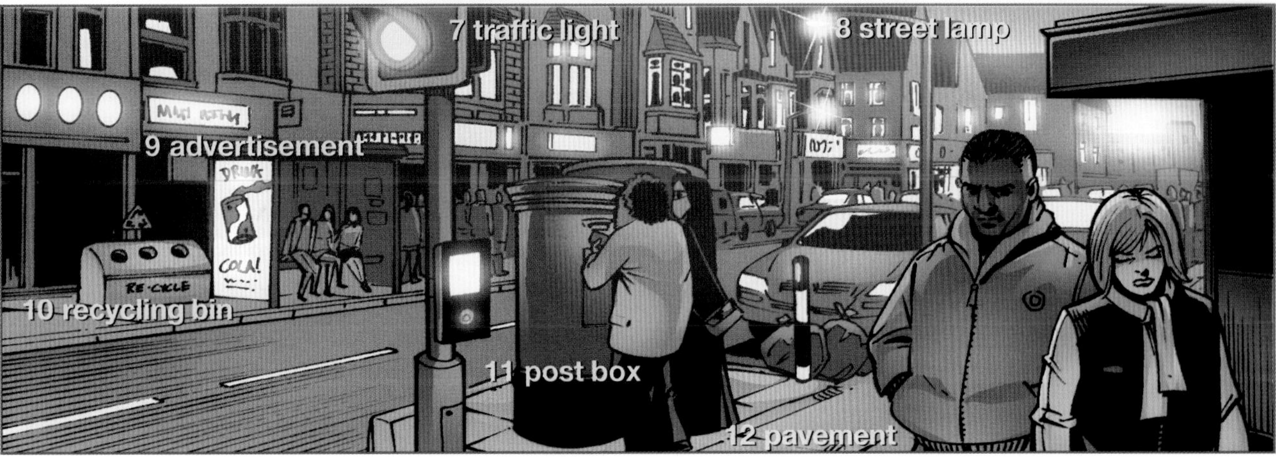

2 Complete the sentences. Use words from exercise 1, singular or plural form.

1 We left our car in the ...... and walked to the town centre.
2 Is there a ...... near here? I need to post this letter.
3 It's very dark in my street at night because there aren't any ....
4 We live in a ...... on the tenth floor.
5 They've just built a new ...... between here and London, so it's quicker to go by car than by train.
6 There was a big ...... for Levi jeans on the side of the bus.
7 'What do they make in that ......?' 'Computers.'
8 The ...... were red, so the bus stopped.
9 I found £10 on the ...... outside the post office.
10 There are lots of ...... across the River Thames in London.

3 Write six sentences about your town or village. Use the words in exercise 1.

There's a motorway near my village.

More practice? Workbook page 77

ABBY'S STORY

New friends

Rachel

Dan

1 Friends are so important. I used to have lots of friends in Liverpool. Then I moved to London and started at this new school. I remember my first day – it was terrible. I wasn't feeling very happy. In fact, I was feeling really lonely. Then Rachel sat next to me, and we started talking. We became friends immediately. We're still good friends – and we often sit and talk for ages!

Abby How did you and Dan start going out?

Rachel He sent me a Valentine's card.

Abby Really? How romantic! How did you guess it was from him?

Rachel He wrote his name in it.

Abby Oh, that's sweet.

Rachel He used to be more romantic. He used to make CDs for me – compilations of his favourite songs. He doesn't do that now.

Abby Well, maybe you've got all his favourite songs.

Rachel And he used to phone me when I was walking to school, just to say hello.

Abby Ssh! Look! Dan's coming into the coffee bar now!

2

1 Read and listen to Abby's story. Did Dan make a CD for Rachel or for Abby?

2 **Correct the sentences.**

1 Abby was feeling cheerful on her first day at her new school.
2 Dan sat next to Abby on her first day at school.
3 Rachel sent Dan a Valentine's card.
4 Dan used to buy CDs for Rachel.
5 Abby asked Dan to make her a CD.

3 **Answer the questions.**

1 Where did Abby live before she moved to London?
2 Why does Abby think that Dan doesn't make Rachel CDs any more?
3 Why did Dan use to phone Rachel?
4 What was Dan doing when he saw Rachel and Abby in the café?
5 Why do you think Rachel looked jealous?

4 **REAL ENGLISH Find equivalents for these sentences in the story.**

1 We often sit and talk for a very long time.
2 That's nice and charming.
3 I wasn't responsible for the problem.

5 **REAL ENGLISH Rewrite the underlined words with expressions from exercise 4.**

1 I lived in Oxford for a very long time.
2 It was nice and charming of him to buy you flowers.
3 You didn't stop at the traffic lights! You were responsible!

What do you think?

Do you agree or disagree with these statements?

- Dan should be more romantic.
- Dan shouldn't make CDs for Abby.
- It's natural that Rachel is jealous.
- Abby shouldn't feel terrible. It isn't her fault.

Vote YES or NO for each one and give your reasons.

Word help

Extreme adjectives

6 **Match each normal adjective in box A with an extreme adjective in box B. Use your dictionary to help you.**

bad – terrible

A Normal adjectives
~~bad~~ beautiful big cold dirty good hot hungry small

B Extreme adjectives
boiling enormous fantastic filthy freezing gorgeous starving ~~terrible~~ tiny

7 **Answer the questions. Use extreme adjectives. Then listen, check and repeat.**

Are you hot? Hot? I'm boiling!
1 Was the concert good?
2 Were his exam results bad?
3 This pizza is a bit small, isn't it?
4 I think Jane is beautiful.
5 That's a big factory.
6 It's a bit cold in here.
7 My shoes are dirty.
8 Are you hungry?

More practice? Workbook page 77

Pronunciation Stress and intonation

1 **Listen and repeat the sentences. Pay attention to the stress and intonation.**

1 I'm starving!
2 That bridge is enormous!

2 **Mark the most important syllable in these sentences. Say them, then listen and check.**

1 Your hands are filthy!
2 It's boiling in here!
3 I think Ben Affleck is gorgeous!
4 The film was terrible!

Past simple and past continuous

1 Study the sentences. Which verbs are in the past simple? Which verbs are in the past continuous?

> Rachel and Abby **became** friends immediately.
> He **sent** me a Valentine's card.
> Rachel and Abbey **were talking** about CDs.
> '**Was** Dan **passing** the coffee bar when he **saw** Rachel inside?' 'Yes, he was.'

2 Complete the rules with past simple and past continuous.

1 We use the .... to talk about completed actions in the past.
2 We use the .... to describe actions that were in progress at a specific time in the past.

3 Listen. What were they doing when their mobiles rang? Write sentences using the past continuous form of the verbs in the box.

chat   listen to the radio   play the guitar   sleep   wash up

1 – When his mobile rang, Hanif was ...

1 Hanif
2 Dan
3 Abby and Rachel
4 Fatima
5 Macey

Take note!

We use the past continuous for a longer action and the past simple for a shorter action that interrupts the longer action.

I **was doing** my homework <u>when</u> my mobile **rang**.
My mobile **rang** <u>while</u> I **was doing** my homework.

We often use *when* with the past simple and *while* with the past continuous.

4 Complete the sentences. Use the past simple and past continuous.

1 We ...... (drive) down the motorway when we ...... (see) the accident.
2 My grandad ...... (go) to sleep while he ...... (watch) TV.
3 It ...... (rain) when we ...... (leave) school.
4 While she ...... (wait) for the bus, somebody ...... (steal) her mobile.
5 Where ...... (John / be) while you ...... (tidy) his room?
6 Where ...... (you / go) when I ...... (see) you in town?

5 Complete the text. Use the past simple or the past continuous.

Moving house

We moved from New York to London last month. It was cold and cloudy when we (**1** arrive) at our new house, but it (**2** not rain). We (**3** not have) any milk in the house, so while my dad and brother (**4** open) boxes, my mum and I (**5** decide) to go out to buy some.

We (**6** cross) the road at the traffic lights, when we (**7** see) an advertisement for a new film about New York. I suddenly (**8** feel) sad about leaving America. Anyway, we (**9** buy) some milk and then (**10** go) home. We (**11** open) our front door when a boy (**12** come) out of the house next door. He (**13** wear) jeans and a trendy jacket. He (**14** say) hello and smiled at me. I immediately (**15** think), 'Maybe my new home isn't so bad!'

More practice? Workbook pages 78–79

Dialogue

1 Read and listen. Which films does Hanif suggest?

a) Gladiator b) Matrix Reloaded c) Troy
d) Notting Hill e) Pirates of the Caribbean

Expressing likes and dislikes

Hanif	What shall we watch?
Abby	Have a look through the DVDs.
Hanif	Oh, you've got *Gladiator*. That's a fantastic film. I like Russell Crowe.
Abby	Do you? I used to really like him, but I've gone off him a bit.
Hanif	What about *Troy*?
Abby	No, I watched it last weekend. How about *Pirates of the Caribbean*? Do you like Johnny Depp?
Hanif	He's not bad.
Abby	He's brilliant in that.
Hanif	Oh, this is good: *Matrix Reloaded*.
Abby	That's my brother's. I'm not very keen on science fiction.
Hanif	Well, what shall we watch, then?
Abby	There's a good film on TV tonight: *Notting Hill*.
Hanif	*Notting Hill*! That's so old! And I can't stand romantic comedies.
Abby	OK. Let's watch *Gladiator*, then.

2 REAL ENGLISH Listen and repeat these expressions. What do they mean?

1 I've gone off him.
2 He's not bad.
3 I'm not very keen on science fiction.
4 I can't stand romantic comedies.

3 Practise reading the dialogue.

4 Write your own dialogue. Choose different films and actors.

A: What shall we watch?
B: Have a look through the DVDs.

5 Act out your dialogue.

More practice? Workbook page 79

Listening

6 Listen to Abby and Dan. Do they have similar or different tastes in music?

7 Listen again. Answer the questions.

1 When did Abby listen to the CD?
2 How many Anastacia songs are there on the CD?
3 Who prefers Anastacia's old style?
4 Did Abby use to like Alicia Keys?
5 What does Abby think of *Linkin Park*?
6 What does Dan think of *Linkin Park*?

GRAMMAR 2

used to

Take note!

We use *used to* to talk about actions or situations that happened regularly in the past but no longer happen.

Abby **used to** live in Liverpool. Now she lives in London.

When I was little, I **didn't use to** like pizza. Now I love it.

When you were at primary school, how **did you use to** get to school?

The forms of *used to* are the same as regular verbs in the past simple.

1 Complete the sentences. Use *used to*, affirmative and negative, and the present simple in each sentence.

1 My dad ...... (work) in a factory, but now he ...... (be) a fire-fighter.
2 There ...... (be) a train station in our town, but there ...... (not be) one any more.
3 We ...... (live) in a block of flats, but we ...... (live) in a house now.
4 There ...... (not be) a motorway near our village, but there ...... (be) one now.
5 When he was little he ...... (love) sweets, but now he ...... (hate) them.
6 Mandy ...... (not like) reading, but now she ...... (read) all the time.

2 Mike is remembering his childhood. Write sentences about him. Use *used to*, affirmative or negative.

1 have a cat
2 have fair hair
3 wear glasses
4 have long hair
5 wear short trousers
6 play computer games

3 Look at the pictures of the shopping street. Write sentences with *There used to be* and *There didn't use to be*.

1 There used to be an amusement arcade.
2 There didn't use to be a bus stop.

1 amusement arcade
2 bus stop
3 traffic lights
4 post box
5 post office
6 internet café
7 video rental shop
8 newsagent's
9 fast-food restaurant

1980

Now

Communicate!

Write five sentences about your town as it used to be.

There used to be lots of factories.
There didn't use to be any supermarkets.

More practice? Workbook pages 78–79

Liverpool City of change

1 Match the pictures (1–4) with the paragraphs (A–D).

2 Read the text. What is the significance of the dates in the box?

1700 1809 1846–50 1880 the 1980s 2008

1700 – In 1700 Liverpool's population was 20,000.

3 Are these sentences true or false? Correct the false ones.

1 Liverpool first became rich because of the slave trade.
2 Slave ships used to sail from Liverpool to the West Indies, then to Africa, then back to Liverpool.
3 Nearly a million Irish people came to Liverpool during the famine.
4 Britain lost her colonies in the 20th century.
5 The buildings in the port are falling down, and Liverpool is still declining.

What does the city of Liverpool make you think of? The famous red shirts and shorts of Liverpool FC, or perhaps *The Beatles*? Liverpool has a fascinating history and it has changed a lot in the last three hundred years ...

A In 1700, Liverpool was a small port with a population of 20,000. By 1800 it was a large, rich city. How did this happen? The answer is: the slave trade. Ships used to sail from Liverpool to Africa and transport slaves to the West Indies to work on the sugar plantations. The ships then brought back sugar to Liverpool. Approximately ten million slaves crossed the Atlantic in this way, until the slave trade became illegal in Britain in 1809.

B In the nineteenth century, ships from Liverpool sailed all over the world transporting steel, cloth and coal to Britain's colonies. The city continued to grow and soon became badly over-crowded. Cholera used to kill thousands every year, and in the 1840s, 25,000 homeless children were living on the streets. Between 1846 and 1850 there was a terrible famine in Ireland. Nearly one million starving Irish people came to Liverpool. Most emigrated to America but 80,000 stayed in the city. By 1880 Liverpool's population was 600,000.

C Industry and trade declined in the twentieth century as Britain lost her colonies. By the 1980s the port was closed, and many of the buildings were falling down. But Liverpool became famous for other things, especially football and music. Britain's most famous pop group, *The Beatles*, came from Liverpool, and by the 1970s Liverpool FC was one of the best teams in the world.

D Today Liverpool is a modern, exciting city. They are restoring the port buildings, and there are lots of new shops, museums and restaurants. It's also 'European City of Culture' for 2008 – and it's still famous for football: Wayne Rooney was born in Liverpool.

4 **WORD CHECK** Find the words (1–4) in the text and match them to the meanings (a–d).

1 slave (line 8)
2 over-crowded (line 18)
3 famine (line 21)
4 declined (line 26)

a) with too many people
b) diminished; got smaller
c) somebody who works for no money and has no freedom
d) a time when there is not enough food

Model text My town, then and now

1 Read the text. Does Mark think life was better now or 50 years ago?

I live in a small town in the south of England. 50 years ago the town was very different.

It was much smaller and most of the buildings were already very old. There didn't use to be any modern buildings. Now there are some blocks of flats. The shops were all small and in the centre of the town. Now people go shopping in big shopping centres outside the town.

Transport is very different too. There used to be a station, but the railway isn't there now. Not many people had cars. They used to travel by bus or train. Now there are more roads, and there's a big motorway just a few miles away.

My grandparents lived in the town 50 years ago. They say that there wasn't much to do then. There was a cinema and a café. The cinema is still there, and now there's an amusement arcade and a sports centre.

In conclusion, life was quieter then, but in my opinion it's better now.

2 Divide the words and phrases from the text into two groups: *50 years ago* and *Now*.

amusement arcade   big shopping centres   blocks of flats   motorway   not much to do   old buildings   small shops   sports centre   station

Structuring an essay

Take note!

- Start your essay with a short introduction, and finish with a short conclusion giving your opinion.
- Divide your essay into paragraphs, each with its own topic.
- Make notes for each topic.

3 Make notes about your city, town or village. Ask your parents, grandparents, or teachers about life 50 years ago. Use these headings.

1 Buildings – now
  Buildings – 50 years ago
2 Transport – now
  Transport – 50 years ago
3 Social life – now
  Social life – 50 years ago

Writing task

4 Use your notes to write about your city, town or village.

Introduction
I live in … 50 years ago …
Paragraph 1: Buildings
It was … There used to be …
There didn't use to be …
Now there are …
Paragraph 2: Transport
People used to travel by …
Now people …
Paragraph 3: Social life
Fifty years ago there was …
People used to … Now there's …
Conclusion
In conclusion, life was …
but in my opinion it's …

More practice? Workbook page 80

Learning Diary page 81

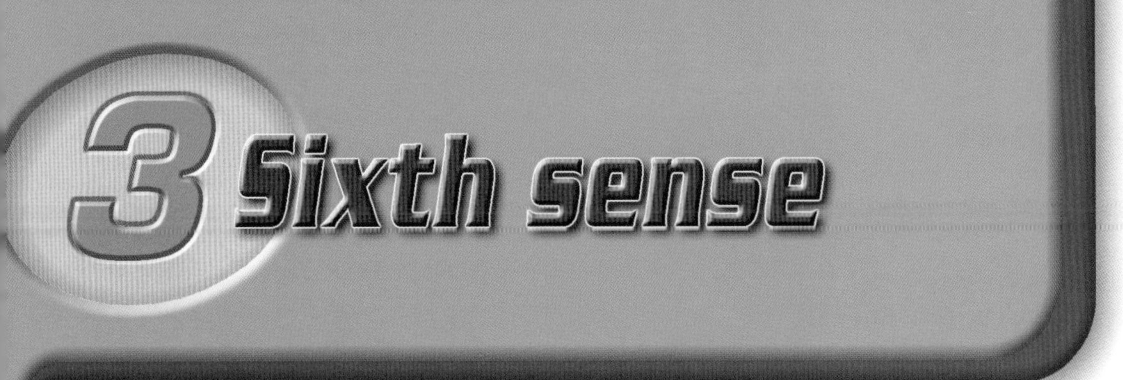

3 Sixth sense

UNIT FOCUS

- The senses
- Words that are verbs and nouns
- Present perfect affirmative and negative
- Present perfect with *just*
- At the doctor's
- Brainstorming

VOCABULARY

The senses

1 Listen and repeat the words. What do they mean?

2 Match the sentences with the five senses in exercise 1.

His voice **sounds** strange – *hearing*

1 That cake **looks** delicious!
2 This jumper **feels** very soft.
3 This cheese **tastes** awful!
4 That perfume **smells** great.

3 Complete the sentences. Use the verbs from exercise 2 and the pictures (1–6).

1 The can *feels cold.*
2 The milk …
3 She …
4 The music …
5 The chocolate …
6 That maths question …

4 In pairs, ask and answer the questions. Use the words in the box.

church bells garlic fresh coffee
hot chocolate the sea the wind in the trees

Do you like the sound of … ?
Do you like the taste of … ?
Do you like the smell of … ?

Do you like the sound of church bells?

Yes, I love it. What about you?

More practice? Workbook page 82

RACHEL'S STORY
Sixth sense?
1 Abby has got a brother called Victor. I haven't met him yet, but I know that they're very close. She called him on his mobile when we were at my house yesterday. He didn't answer. She immediately knew that something was wrong – I don't know how, but she had a feeling.
Abby
Macey
Maybe he's somewhere noisy and can't hear it.
No, Macey. Something's wrong. I know it. I'm phoning home.
2 She phoned home and spoke to her mum. Her mum told her that Victor was fine.
He's just gone out on his bike.
Maybe he hasn't taken his phone with him.
3 We carried on chatting, but Abby was still worried. Then she got a call from her mum. Victor wasn't OK after all. Her feeling was correct.
He's had an accident on his bike. Mum has just spoken to the doctor at the hospital.
4
Hi Dan
Have you heard about Abby's brother, Victor? He had an accident on his bike. He's OK though. He's already left hospital. I was with Abby when it happened, and she knew that something was wrong. It was weird – intuition, a sixth sense, whatever. I didn't use to believe in things like that, but I've changed my mind now!
Rachel x

1 Read and listen to Rachel's story. Explain why the sentences are false.

1 Rachel knows Victor very well.
2 Victor had a very serious accident.
3 Rachel has always believed in a sixth sense.

2 Put the events of the story in the correct order.

a) Victor didn't answer his phone.
b) Abby's mum called Abby and told her about the accident.
c) Abby called Victor.
d) Rachel sent an email to Dan.
e) Abby's mum said Victor was fine.
f) Victor left hospital.
g) Abby called her mum and asked about Victor.
h) Abby's mum spoke to the doctor.

3 **REAL ENGLISH** Find equivalents for these sentences in the story.

1 We continued chatting.
2 Her mum phoned her.
3 It was very strange.
4 I've got a different opinion now.

4 **REAL ENGLISH** Rewrite the underlined words with expressions from exercise 3.

1 I'm so tired. I can't continue!
2 My best friend phoned me this morning.
3 My brother often says very strange things.
4 Do you still believe in ghosts, or have you got a different opinion now?

What do you think?

Do you agree or disagree with these statements?

- It was just a coincidence that Abby felt that something was wrong.
- I believe in a sixth sense.

Vote YES or NO for each one and give your reasons.

Word help

Words that are verbs and nouns

Take note!

Some words can be both a verb and a noun: for example, *answer*.

5 Decide if the bold words in these sentences are verbs or nouns.

1 These sandwiches **taste** awful!
2 Can I use your **phone**?
3 I didn't **touch** your computer!
4 Did you enjoy your **visit** to the museum?
5 I think **love** is more important than money.

6 Complete the sentences. Use the same word in each pair of sentences, once as a verb and once as a noun.

break chat rain smell walk work

1 a) Those flowers ...... wonderful!
b) I don't like the ...... of this coffee!
2 a) I need some fresh air. Let's go for a ....
b) I always ...... to school.
3 a) We sit and ...... for hours.
b) I had a good ...... with my friend last night.
4 a) It started to ...... an hour ago.
b) Don't go out in the ...... – you'll get wet.
5 a) She's very busy. She's got a lot of ...... to do.
b) My new computer doesn't ....
6 a) Did you drop your glasses and ...... them?
b) We always have a five-minute ...... between lessons.

More practice? Workbook page 82

Pronunciation Consonant clusters

1 Listen and repeat.

Spain smile stop slow school

2 Listen and repeat the tongue twisters. Practise them.

1 The Spanish skater spoke slowly.
2 I saw a Scottish sports star at the station.

GRAMMAR 1

Present perfect affirmative and negative

1 Study the table.

Affirmative	Negative
I've finished You've finished He/She/It's finished We've finished You've finished They've finished	I haven't finished You haven't finished He/She/It hasn't finished We haven't finished You haven't finished They haven't finished

We use the present perfect to talk about:
1 an action that happened in the past that has a connection with the present.
2 an experience.

Take note!

The past participle of regular verbs is the same as the past simple form.

Past simple	**Past participle**
watched	watched
carried	carried
chatted	chatted

2 Find the past participles of these irregular verbs in the list on page 56.

Base form	Past simple	Past participle
be	was/were	been
break	broke	1 ......
do	did	2 ......
have	had	3 ......
hear	heard	4 ......
know	knew	5 ......
leave	left	6 .....
meet	met	7 ......
put	put	8 ......
sleep	slept	9 ......
take	took	10 ......

Take note!

We usually use *been* as the past participle of *go*.
He's **been** snowboarding.

3 Complete the sentences. Use the present perfect affirmative, and the verbs in the box.

break finish ~~go~~ have hear leave walk write

My brother has been hang-gliding – he loved it!
1 I'm not very hungry because I ...... lunch.
2 He ...... ten kilometres today, so he's really tired.
3 We ...... our homework, so we can go out now.
4 I ...... an email to my girlfriend but I haven't sent it.
5 Look. John ...... his money on the table.
6 I ...... this song before, but I can't remember the name of the singer.
7 We can't use this printer now – you ...... it!

Watch out!

We can't use past time expressions with the present perfect.
~~I've been skateboarding yesterday.~~ ✗
I **went** skateboarding **yesterday**. ✔
When we use the present perfect, the time of the action is not important, or we don't know the time of the action.
I've **been** skateboarding. (= at some time in the past).

4 Write sentences. Use the present perfect negative.

1 I / not try / parachuting
2 this lesson / not be / boring
3 he / not meet / Cameron Diaz
4 you / not do / the washing
5 they / not sleep / all night
6 she / not take / any photos

Dialogue

1 Read and listen. What problem does Dan have?

At the doctor's

Doctor	Hello, Dan. What's the problem?
Dan	I've got earache.
Doctor	When did it start?
Dan	Three days ago.
Doctor	Let me have a look … Ah, yes, you've got an infection. Have you taken any medication for it?
Dan	Just some painkillers.
Doctor	OK. I'll prescribe some antibiotics. Take them three times a day. Come back and see me again when you've finished them.
Dan	OK. Thank you, doctor.

2 **REAL ENGLISH** Listen and repeat these expressions. What do they mean?

1 What's the problem?
2 I've got earache.
3 Three days ago.
4 Let me have a look.

3 Practise reading the dialogue.

4 Write your own dialogue. Use the ideas in the box or invent your own.

a sore throat	sore eyes	a cough

A: Hello, … What's the problem?
B: I've got …

5 Act out your dialogue.

More practice? Workbook page 84

Listening

6 Listen to Victor and Abby. Has Victor broken his arm?

7 Listen again. Choose *a* or *b*.

1 What happened as Victor was going past the traffic lights?
a) A car hit him. **b)** A car nearly hit him.
2 Why didn't the car stop at the traffic lights?
a) The driver didn't see the light.
b) The light was green.
3 How did the driver feel after the accident?
a) She was angry. **b)** She was worried.
4 What car was she driving?
a) A big BMW. **b)** A small Mercedes.
5 Why didn't they call an ambulance?
a) Victor said he was OK.
b) They couldn't find a phone box.
6 Why did the woman wait for Victor at the hospital?
a) His bike was in her car.
b) She was worried about his bike.

Present perfect revision

1 **Which sports have Rod, Sue and Tim done before? Write sentences. Use the present perfect affirmative or negative.**

Rod has been snorkelling.

		Rod	Sue & Tim
1		✔	✗
2		✗	✔
3		✗	✔
4		✔	✗
5		✔	✗
6		✗	✔

2 **Which sports have *you* done? Write sentences about the sports in the box. Use the present perfect affirmative or negative.**

I've been cycling. I haven't been ...

cycling mountain biking rock-climbing rollerblading skateboarding skiing snorkelling snowboarding swimming windsurfing

More practice? Workbook pages 83–84

Present perfect with *just*

Take note!

We often use *just* with the present perfect to talk about very recent actions or events. We put *just* between *have/has* and the past participle.

Oh no, we can't go rollerblading. It's ***just*** *started to rain!*

3 **Look at the pictures and write sentences. Use *just* and the present perfect affirmative.**

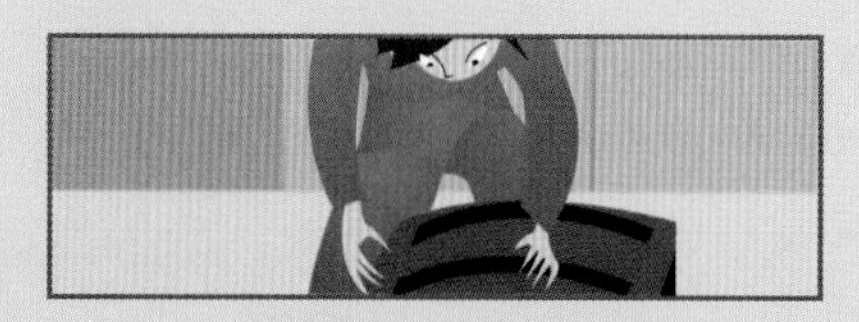

she / check / her parachute
She's just checked her parachute.

1 she / get on / the plane

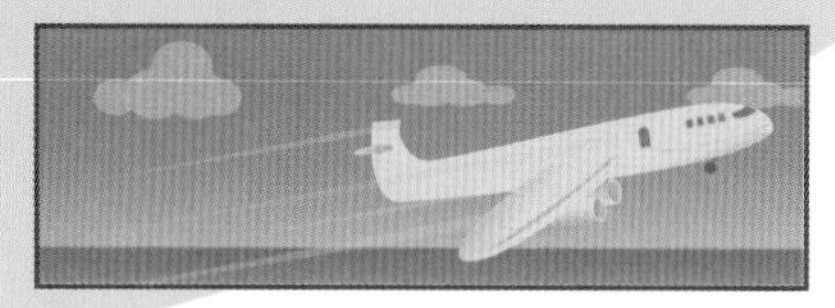

2 the plane / take off

3 she / put on / her helmet

4 she / jump out of / the plane

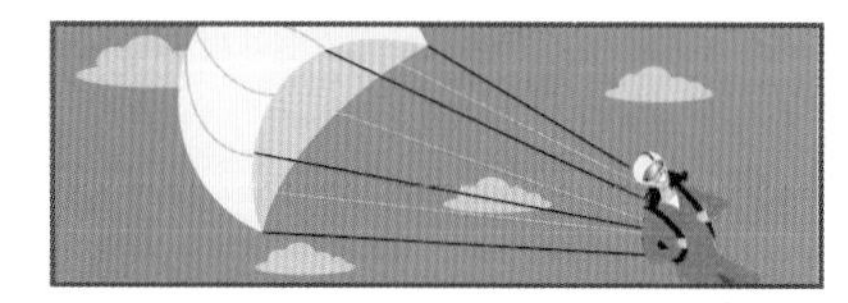

5 her parachute / open

6 she / land

Communicate!

Write four sentences about things you've done or haven't done today.
I've had a maths lesson.
I haven't watched TV.

More practice? Workbook pages 83–84

1 Read the text. Which sentence is true?

a) Everybody with synaesthesia can 'see' sounds. for example, they see colours when they hear music.
b) Everybody with synaesthesia can 'taste' words.
c) Everybody with synaesthesia has unusual connections between their senses.

Synaesthesia

What colour is the number 'eight'? Does a square taste sweet or salty? Have you ever felt the colour 'green'? For most people, these questions don't make sense. They don't 'feel' colours or 'taste' shapes. But some people experience the world differently, and their senses are interconnected in unusual ways. This is known as synaesthesia.

Jennifer and Catherine Strutt are twins from Australia. They have a form of synaesthesia in which sounds and colours are mixed. For example, they see colours when they listen to music. For Catherine, the sound of a double bass is dark green or purple. For Jennifer, flutes, clarinets and other wind instruments are light blue.

Scientists have found that about one in every 100 people has synaesthesia, and that it's common among artists, poets and musicians. Many of the people who have it probably haven't realised yet. They might think that everybody sees the colour yellow when they think of the number 'seven'.

Associating colours with sounds, numbers or letters is the most common form of synaesthesia, but there are other kinds. James Wannerton from the north of England has always associated certain words with certain tastes. He can't help it: when he hears the word, he automatically experiences the taste in his mouth. For example, the word 'exactly' always tastes of yoghurt, and the word 'knowledge' always tastes of sausage sandwiches.

James's condition has brought problems. It's difficult to concentrate when you're experiencing so many different tastes. It has caused problems in relationships too. Some names have specific tastes for James. He's sometimes found it difficult to like a person if their name tastes bad!

2 Read the text again. Answer the questions.

1 What is different about people with synaesthesia?
2 For Jennifer Strutt, which instruments are light blue?
3 How many people in the world have synaesthesia?
4 How could people not realise they have synaesthesia?
5 What is the most common form of synaesthesia?
6 What word tastes of yoghurt to James Wannerton?
7 Why is it difficult for James to concentrate?
8 Why has James's synaesthesia made it difficult for him to like some people?

3 **WORD CHECK** Find words in the text that mean:

1 geometric forms – squares, triangles, etc.
2 brothers or sisters born on the same day
3 a blue-red colour
4 making a connection between
5 immediately, without thinking

WRITING

Model text Personal memories

1 Read the text. Do any of these smells or sounds have associations for you too?

Do some smells remind you of your childhood? What associations do they have?
The smell of crayons reminds me of when I was about five years old. I used to love drawing. I've always liked the smell of suntan lotion because it reminds me of holidays at the beach. If I close my eyes and smell the bottle, I can imagine being on holiday! I also love the smell of fireworks because they make me think of festivals and special occasions, like Bonfire Night.

What about sounds? Do some sounds or songs have strong associations for you - positive or negative?
Yes, certain songs bring back memories. For example, there's a McFly song called *Obviously*. It was on the radio all the time in the summer of 2004. That was a really good summer for me, because I made lots of new friends and had a great time. So when I hear that song now, I feel happy. Also, any song by Robbie Williams makes me think of my girlfriend, because she's a big fan of his music and has made me listen to all his CDs!

2 Match the smells and sounds (1–5) with their associations (a–e).

1 crayons	a) beach holidays
2 the song *Obviously*	b) summer 2004
3 any Robbie Williams song	c) being five years old
4 suntan lotion	d) special occasions
5 fireworks	e) his girlfriend

Brainstorming

Take note!

Make notes before you begin writing. You don't need to write complete sentences. Then decide which ideas you want to include.

smell of cigarettes – my grandfather
pizza – holiday in Italy
Britney Spears songs – my friend Sam

3 Make notes about your own 'sense connections'. Use these headings.

1 Smells with associations
What they remind me of
2 Sounds or songs with associations
What they remind me of

Writing task

4 Use your notes to write a text. Use the writing guide to help you.

Paragraph 1
Do some smells remind you of your childhood? What associations do they have?
The smell of ... reminds me of ...
I also like the smell of ... because it makes me think of ...
Paragraph 2
What about sounds? Do some sounds or songs have strong associations for you – positive or negative?
Certain songs/sounds bring back ... For example, ...
When I hear ... I feel ...
When I hear ... I think of ...

More practice? Workbook page 85

Learning Diary page 86

Revision: Units 1–3

VOCABULARY

Describing appearance

1 Complete the description. Use the words in the box.

bracelet dyed hair make-up necklaces piercing rings scruffy sunglasses

She's wearing pink (**1**) ...... and a (**2**) ...... pink T-shirt. She's got green and blue (**3**) .... She's got a (**4**) ...... on her arm and a (**5**) ...... in her nose. She's wearing lots of (**6**) ...... , (**7**) ...... around her neck and (**8**) ...... on her fingers.

-ed and *-ing* adjectives

2 Complete the adjectives. Use *-ed* or *-ing*.

1 I only got 30% in my history exam. I was very disappoint..... .
2 Horror films are really frighten..... .
3 I fell over in the classroom. It was really embarrass..... .
4 I'm bor.... ! Let's do something excit..... .
5 I'm surpris .... that you think the film was bor..... . I think it was really interest..... .
6 I thought I put my keys in my bag but they aren't there. I'm confus..... .

The urban landscape

3 Complete the words. Use *a*, *e*, *i*, *o* and *u*.

1 f_ct_ry
2 br_dg_
3 bl_ck _f fl_ts
4 r__lw_y
5 m_t_rw_y
6 p_v_m_nt
7 tr_ff_c l_ghts
8 r_cycl_ng b_ns
9 str__t l_mp
10 _dv_rt_s_m_nt

Extreme adjectives

4 Write the extreme adjectives.

1 hot – b......
2 big – e......
3 dirty – f......
4 cold – f......
5 beautiful – g......
6 hungry – s......
7 bad – t......
8 small – t......

The senses

5 Label the five senses.

6 Complete the sentences. Use the correct form of *feel*, *look*, *smell*, *sound* and *taste*.

1 This music ...... strange.
2 Is Tim OK? He ...... really worried.
3 Your hands ...... cold. Do you want to borrow my gloves?
4 This soup ...... horrible!
5 Dogs ...... awful when they're wet.

Words that are verbs and nouns

7 Complete the sentences with the words in the box. Then decide whether they are verbs or nouns in the sentences.

answer ~~phone~~ rain smell visit walk work

Can you phone later? (verb)
1 I'm going to ...... my cousin in Chile.
2 I hate the ...... of bananas.
3 I'm confused. What's the ...... to this question?
4 My dad spends a lot of time at ....
5 'Shall we take the bus?' 'No, let's ....'
6 Quick! Let's go in. It's starting to ....

GRAMMAR

Present tense contrast

1 Complete the sentences. Use the present simple in one sentence and the present continuous in the other.

1 a) 'What ...... you ...... (do)?' 'I'm a student.'
  b) 'What ...... you ...... (do)?' 'I ....' (read)
2 a) Look. Mark ...... (wear) a really trendy jacket.
  b) Why ...... he always ...... (wear) those funny sunglasses?
3 a) We ...... (not live) in a block of flats.
  b) He ...... (live) in York while he's at university.
4 a) Be quiet! I ...... (listen) to the radio.
  b) I ...... (not listen) to the radio in bed.
5 a) The traffic lights are green. Why ...... that car ...... (not move)?
  b) 150,000 people ...... (move) to London every year.

2 Complete the sentences with the verbs in the box. Use the present simple or the present continuous.

do hate know not remember rain read wear

1 I ...... a really good book. Do you want to read it after me?
2 Look! That man ...... a Chelsea shirt here in Liverpool.
3 Oh dear. We can't go to the beach. It ....
4 I ...... who he is, but I ...... his name.
5 'What ...... she ...... ?' 'She's a teacher.'
6 Rachel ...... playing computer games.

like/hate, etc. + gerund

3 Write true sentences. Use *love*, *enjoy*, *don't mind*, *like*, *don't like* or *hate* + gerund.

1 – I hate eating late at night.

1 eat late at night
2 watch advertisements on TV
3 wear scruffy clothes
4 travel by train
5 walk home in the rain
6 wash my hair
7 go to bed early
8 pay for my mobile phone bill

Subject and object questions

4 Write questions. Use *who* or *what*.

Somebody is wearing perfume.
Who is wearing perfume?
He lost something.
What did he lose?

1 Somebody is waiting on the pavement.
2 She smelt something.
3 Something fell out of his pocket.
4 Somebody followed her.
5 He said something.
6 They saw somebody in the car park.

Past simple and past continuous

5 Write sentences. Use the past simple and the past continuous, affirmative, negative or interrogative.

when / we / see / Jake, / he / play football / in the park.
When we saw Jake, he was playing football in the park.

1 it / not rain / when / I / go out.
2 where / she / go / when / she / have / the accident?
3 I / see / them / while / I / put / bottles / in the recycling bin.
4 why / you / not do / your homework / when / I / get home?
5 she / not feel / very happy / when / she / leave / school.

used to

6 **Write sentences about Kate when she was younger. Match items (1–6) with (a–f). Use *used to*, affirmative or negative.**

1 – d She didn't use to walk to school.

1	not walk	a)	dyed hair
2	live	b)	earrings
3	not wear	c)	in a block of flats
4	share	d)	to school
5	not have	e)	volleyball
6	play	f)	a room with her sister

Present perfect (affirmative and negative)

7 **Look at the list. Write sentences about what Rick has and hasn't done today. Use the present perfect, affirmative and negative.**

1 He hasn't done his homework.

1 do my homework ✗
2 phone Sally ✓
3 have a shower ✓
4 send text message to Ben ✗
5 tidy my room ✗
6 buy the new Darkness CD ✗
7 wash the dishes ✓

Present perfect with *just*

8 **Look at the pictures. Write sentences with the present perfect affirmative and *just*. Use the verbs in the box.**

arrive fall off finish get up ~~land~~
leave see win

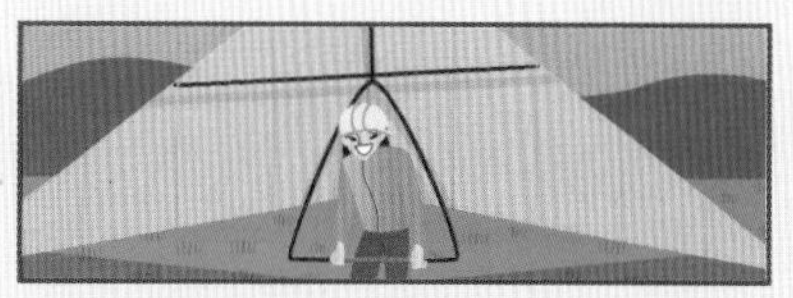

She's just landed.

1 She ...... a shark.

2 He ......

3 She ...... the house.

4 He ...... his skateboard.

5 He ...... his lunch.

6 They ...... the match.

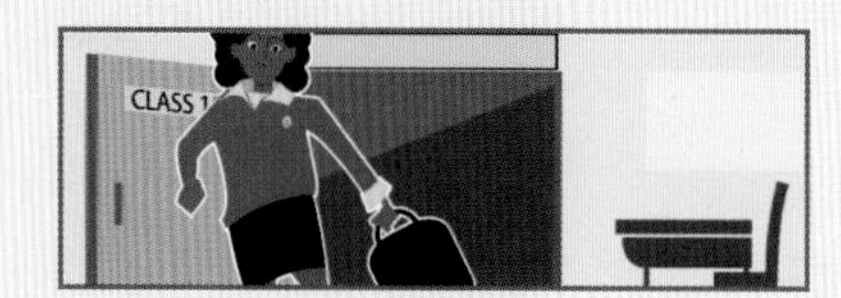

7 She ...... in class.

Build up: Units 1–3

1 Complete the text. Choose the correct words.

1 a) I'm enjoying b) I enjoy
2 a) am thinking b) think
3 a) wearing b) wear
4 a) Did you have b) Do you had
5 a) did go b) went
6 a) did you see b) you saw
7 a) Are you believing b) Do you believe
8 a) was thinking b) thought
9 a) was ringing b) rang
10 a) Are you remembering
b) Do you remember
11 a) was going b) used to go
12 a) has made b) makes
13 a) heard b) hear
14 a) has just b) is

Dear Daisy

How are you? We arrived here in Manchester last Saturday. Everything is fine and **(1)** *...... my new school. I often* **(2)** *...... about you and all my other friends in London. I miss you all!*

Thanks for your letter, and thank you very much for the bracelet. I love **(3)** *...... it. It's so beautiful.*

(4) *...... a good time at the cinema last night? Who* **(5)** *......? What* **(6)** *......? I want to know everything!*

(7) *...... in a sixth sense? Maybe it was just a coincidence, but while I* **(8)** *...... about Max yesterday evening, my phone* **(9)** *...... and it was him! It was great to talk to him. I really miss him.*

Anyway, he told me about his friend Rob. **(10)** *...... Rob? He* **(11)** *...... to our school, but now he lives in New York. Anyway, Rob* **(12)** *...... a CD! He's only 17! It's called 'First Things First'. Max has* **(13)** *...... some of the songs, but he hasn't bought a copy of the CD. I'm sure it's fantastic.*

I must go. My mum **(14)** *...... called me. Dinner's ready.*

Speak to you soon!

Love

Hannah

2 Answer the questions.

1 Which city does Hannah live in now?
2 Where did she use to live?
3 What was she doing when Max phoned?
4 Where does Rob live?
5 What is the name of Rob's CD?
6 Has Max bought Rob's CD?

3 Correct the mistakes.

She **wears** a necklace at the moment. ✗
She's wearing a necklace at the moment. ✓
1 My brother **is playing** chess every evening. ✗
2 **I'm knowing** that girl. She's at my school. ✗
3 I don't mind **to stay** at home tonight. ✗
4 Who **did give** you that CD? ✗
5 I was reading a magazine when Elizabeth **was arriving**. ✗
6 He had a shower. Then he **was going** out. ✗
7 My parents **used live** in Edinburgh. ✗
8 We've **bought just** a new car. ✗
9 Have you **finish** your homework? ✗
10 She's **isn't** been rock-climbing. ✗

UNIT FOCUS

- Relationships and dating
- Noun endings: *-ion* and *-ment*
- Present perfect interrogative
- *for* and *since*
- *How long ... ?*
- At a restaurant
- *both ... and ...*, *neither ... nor ...*

VOCABULARY

Relationships and dating

1 Listen and repeat the phrases in the box. What do they mean?

meet somebody fancy somebody ask somebody out go out with somebody fall in love have an argument split up make up get engaged get married

2 Read the story. Match six of the underlined phrases with the pictures.

Joe met Ellen at a party at a friend's house in July 1999. He fancied her the first moment he saw her. They chatted and danced together. At the end of the evening, Joe asked Ellen out. They went out for six months and fell in love. Then they had an argument and split up. But a week later they made up and they started going out again. A year later they got engaged and in the summer, they got married. They are very happy together.

3 Look at the pictures and write the story of Pete and Hannah.

4 Listen. Compare your story with the story on the recording.

More practice? Workbook page 87

DAN'S STORY

A difficult relationship

Hanif

Fatima

1 **Is it always wrong to lie? I used to think it was, but some situations are really difficult. Last weekend, I was having a discussion with Hanif about his sister, Fatima ...**

Hanif She isn't getting on very well with Dad at the moment. They've had a lot of arguments.
Dan What about?
Hanif Well, she started going out with a boy called Lewis a few weeks ago.
Dan And your dad doesn't like him?
Hanif He's never met him. That isn't the problem. Dad doesn't want Fatima to go out with anyone yet. He wants her to concentrate on her exams.
Dan So what happened?
Hanif He stopped Fatima from seeing Lewis.
Dan She's nearly eighteen!
Hanif I know, but Dad is really protective.
Dan I'm lucky Rachel's dad isn't like that!
Hanif How long have you and Rachel been together?
Dan We've been a couple for more than a year now – since last February.
Hanif Wow! That's ages.

2 **At that moment, Hanif's sister Fatima came up to us. She smiled, but she didn't look relaxed. Then she explained why she was nervous. She was going for a meal with Lewis!**

3 **Hanif agreed to help his sister, but that night, I got an email from him.**

1 Read and listen to Dan's story. Which relationship does the story title refer to? Think of two possible answers.

2 Answer the questions.

1 Who has Fatima started going out with?
2 Why doesn't Fatima's dad want her to go out with Lewis?
3 When did Dan and Rachel start going out?
4 Who does Fatima's dad think she's with?
5 Why is Hanif's dad angry with Hanif?

3 Complete the sentences with the correct names.

1 ...... stopped her from seeing Lewis.
2 ...... is nearly eighteen.
3 ...... is really protective.
4 ...... agreed to help Fatima.
5 ...... got an email from Hanif that night.

4 **REAL ENGLISH** Find equivalents for these sentences in the story.

1 She hasn't got a very good relationship with her dad.
2 How long have you and Rachel been going out?
3 Fatima came towards us.
4 Now Fatima isn't allowed to go out.

5 **REAL ENGLISH** Rewrite the underlined words with expressions from exercise 4.

1 I really like Tom, but I haven't got a very good relationship with his girlfriend.
2 My girlfriend and I have been going out for three months.
3 She came towards me in the street and started to chat.
4 I failed my exams so I'm not allowed to go out.

What do you think?

Do you agree or disagree with these statements?

- Fatima was wrong to disobey her father.
- Fatima's dad is too protective.
- Hanif was wrong to lie to his dad.

Vote YES or NO for each one and give your reasons.

Word help

Noun endings: *-ion* and *-ment*

Take note!

Some nouns are formed by adding *-ion* or *-ment* to verbs.

discuss – discussion
arrange – arrangement

Watch out!

Sometimes the spelling changes.

translate – translation argue – argument

6 Make the verbs in the box into nouns. Use a dictionary if necessary.

advertise announce calculate celebrate collect disappoint embarrass entertain invent pollute

7 Complete the sentences. Use nouns from exercise 6 and the *Watch out!* box.

1 There's an ...... in the newspaper for a new coffee bar.
2 Can you help with this ...... ? I'm not very good at maths.
3 Film, TV and music are all forms of ....
4 He's got an enormous ...... of books.
5 She had an ...... with her mum and now she's grounded.
6 I think the internet was the most important ...... of the twentieth century.

More practice? Workbook page 87

Pronunciation Verb endings: *-aught* and *-ought*

1 Do you know the past participles of these irregular verbs? Check the Irregular verbs list on page 56.

bring buy catch fight teach think

2 Listen and repeat. How are the *-ought* and *-aught* endings pronounced?

GRAMMAR 1

Present perfect interrogative

1 Copy and complete the table.

Interrogative
Have I finished? (1) ...... you finished? (2) ...... he/she/it finished? Have we finished? Have you finished? (3) ...... they finished?
Short answers Yes, I have. / No, I haven't. Yes, she has. / No, she (4) .... Yes, they (5) .... / No, they haven't.

2 What has pop star Ricky Rich done today? Look at the picture and write questions and answers. Use the present perfect.

have / a swim
Has he had a swim? Yes, he has.

1 have / lunch?
2 drink / the champagne?
3 get dressed?
4 read the newspaper?
5 smoke / his cigar?
6 phone / his manager?

3 In pairs, ask and answer about things you have done today. Use the present perfect.

watch / TV
Have you ... ?

1 learn / a lot?
2 have / a maths lesson?
3 eat / anything?
4 use / a computer?
5 chat / to your friends?

More practice? Workbook pages 88–89

for and *since*

4 Study the examples and complete the rules. Use *for* and *since*.

I've been in London **for** three days. I've been in London **since** Tuesday.

1 We use ...... with a period of time.
2 We use ...... with a point in time.

5 Complete the text. Use *for* and *since*.

Star School

Fiona is on holiday in Scotland. She's staying at Star School, a special academy for young actors and singers. She's been there (**1**) ...... last Saturday. She's wanted to come to Star School (**2**) ...... years, and now her dream has come true.

Fiona has had music and drama lessons every day (**3**) ...... she arrived. Her teachers are Kirsty and Malcolm. They've only been the owners of Star School (**4**) ...... 1998, but they've been teachers (**5**) ...... more than twenty years. Fiona hopes they can help her become a star!

Dialogue

1 Read and listen. Complete the dialogue with the words in the box.

drink juice mushroom order please yet

At a restaurant

Waitress	Can I take your (**1**) ...... ?
Fatima	Sorry, I haven't made up my mind yet.
Lewis	Oh, OK. I'll go first. What's the soup of the day?
Waitress	It's (**2**) .... soup.
Lewis	OK, I'll have the soup to start, followed by the chicken, please.
Waitress	Fine. Anything to (**3**) ...... ?
Lewis	Just water, please.
Waitress	Sparkling or still?
Lewis	Sparkling, (**4**) ....
Waitress	Fine. And have you decided (**5**) ...... ?
Fatima	Yes, I have. I'll have the tomato and avocado salad to start, followed by the vegetable lasagne.
Waitress	And to drink?
Fatima	Orange (**6**) ...... , please.
Waitress	OK, I'll bring your drinks shortly.

2 REAL ENGLISH Listen and repeat these expressions. What do they mean?

1 I haven't made up my mind yet.
2 I'll go first.
3 I'll have the soup to start ...
4 ... followed by the chicken, please.

3 Practise reading the dialogue.

4 Write your own dialogue. Choose different food from the menu.

A: Can I take your order?
B: I haven't made up my mind yet.
C: Oh, OK. I'll go ...

Menu

Starters
- Soup of the day
- Tomato and avocado salad
- Grilled sardines
- Garlic prawns

Main courses
- Grilled chicken with fries and salad
- Beef and mushroom pie with mashed potato and vegetables
- Roast cod with new potatoes and green beans
- Vegetable lasagne

5 Act out your dialogue.

More practice? Workbook page 89

Listening

6 Listen. Match three of these complaints to dialogues 1–3.

a) I didn't order this.
b) The sardines smell bad.
c) I don't like this table.
d) I've waited too long.

7 Listen again. Answer the questions.

Dialogue 1
1 Why doesn't the customer like her table?
2 What's wrong with the table next to the plant?

Dialogue 2
3 Why can't the customer eat chicken?
4 What did she order?

Dialogue 3
5 What did the man have as a starter?
6 How long has he waited for his main course?

Revision: *for* and *since*

1 **Rewrite the sentences with *for* or *since* and the verb in brackets.**

Lucy became ill three days ago. (be)
Lucy has been ill for three days.

1 Lina went to Rosario on Monday. (be)
2 Dave bought that CD player six months ago. (have)
3 We arrived here at five o'clock. (be)
4 Chris came to this school three years ago. (be)
5 I came to this town five years ago. (live)
6 She met Mark in February. (know)

How long ...?

2 **In pairs, write questions. Use *How long* and the present perfect.**

have / these shoes?
How long have you had these shoes?

1 be / at this school?
2 live / in this town?
3 study / English?
4 know / your best friend?

3 **In pairs, ask and answer the questions in exercise 2. Use *for* or *since* in the answer.**

How long have you had those shoes?

I've had them for... / since ...

4 **American rapper MC Rex is visiting London. Complete the radio interview. Use the present perfect affirmative, negative and interrogative. Then listen and check.**

Interviewer Hello, MC Rex. Welcome to the show.
MC Rex Hi. Thank you.
Interviewer Is this your first time in London?
MC Rex I (**1** visit) Britain before, but, no, I (**2** not be) in London.
Interviewer How long (**3** you / be) here?
MC Rex Since Thursday. I'm having a great time. There's so much to see!
Interviewer What (**4** you / see) so far?
MC Rex Well, I (**5** visit) Buckingham Palace and the Tower of London.
Interviewer (**6** you / be) on the London Eye?
MC Rex No, I (**7**) …… , but I'd like to.
Interviewer You should. It's fantastic. (**8** you / see) the model of yourself at Madame Tussauds?
MC Rex Yes, I (**9**) …… . It was perfect!
Interviewer How many concerts (**10** you / play)?
MC Rex I (**11** not play) any. The first concert is this evening. You can watch it on TV.
Interviewer Great. I will!

More practice? Workbook pages 88–89

1 Look at the photos. Do you recognise the singers? Are they successful in your country?

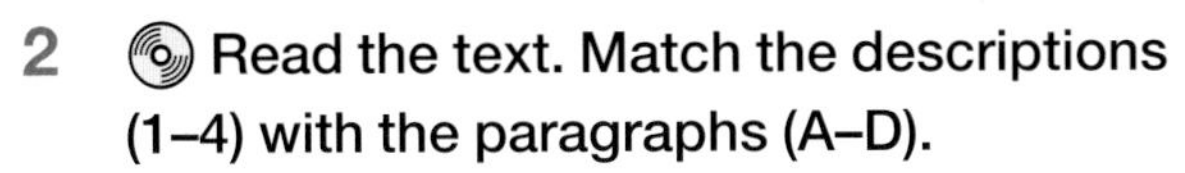

2 Read the text. Match the descriptions (1–4) with the paragraphs (A–D).

1. a split-up that was full of arguments
2. a split-up that was full of love and emotion
3. a split-up that was the start of a successful solo career
4. how being in a pop group is like being in a relationship

SPLITTING UP IS HARD TO DO

A The end of a relationship is a sad and difficult time. This is true for all kinds of relationships, not just couples. Pop groups spend so much time together that the members of the group often become very close. But nothing lasts forever. People leave to start a new career, or there are arguments and the group splits up. It isn't always a sad time, but it's always emotional.

B *Westlife* were one of the most successful groups in the history of pop music. They sold more than thirty million CDs in five years and had twelve number 1 singles. But at a press conference in 2004, there was a dramatic announcement: Brian McFadden was leaving the group. Kian Egan started to read a letter to Brian from the rest of the group. It began: 'We have shared our dreams for five years.' As he was reading the letter, Kian began to cry and couldn't continue. According to the group, there were no arguments: Brian simply wanted to spend more time with his family.

C Other split-ups have been more bitter. The girl group *3LW* (*Three Little Women*) became successful about six years ago. However, one month before the release of their second album, the three girls had an argument. According to one group member, Naturi Naughton, the other two girls threw food at her – fried chicken and potatoes. Naturi left the group. The other two girls have always denied Naturi's accusations.

D When groups split up, the members often try to have careers as solo artists. Since the boy band *Take That!* split up in 1996, Robbie Williams has become one of the most successful and famous singers ever. Splitting up is always hard, but sometimes it's the right decision!

3 Read the text again. Answer the questions.

1. What groups were these people in?
   a) Robbie Williams b) Brian McFadden
   c) Naturi Naughton d) Kian Egan
2. Why do members of pop groups often become very close?
3. According to the group, why did Brian McFadden leave *Westlife*?
4. When did *3LW* become successful?
5. When did *Take That!* split up?

4 **WORD CHECK** Find adjectives in the text from these nouns.

1. emotion (paragraph A)
2. success (paragraph B)
3. drama (paragraph B)
4. fame (paragraph D)

Model text History of a relationship

1 Read the text. How long have Brad and Jennifer known each other? Give answers with *for* and *since.*

Brad Pitt was born in 1963 in Oklahoma, USA. Neither his mother nor his father were actors, but Brad loved films from an early age. He didn't finish high school, but instead moved to California to become an actor. He got his first film role in 1991.

In January 1997, Brad got engaged to his girlfriend, actress Gwyneth Paltrow, but the couple split up later that year.

Jennifer Aniston was born in 1969 in California, USA. Her father was an actor, and Jennifer started acting when she was at school. She got her first small TV role in 1989, but she's been very successful since her role as Rachel in *Friends*.

In 1995, Jennifer started dating actor Tate Donovan, but they split up three years later in 1998.

Brad and Jennifer have known each other since 1998, when they met and fell in love. They got married in July 2000, but the marriage ended in 2005. Both Brad and Jennifer have said that they are still good friends.

2 Copy and complete the chart.

	Brad	Jennifer
Born?		
Parents actors?		
First role?		
Previous relationship?		
Got married?		

both ... and ..., neither ... nor ...

Take note!

Both Brad **and** Jennifer are famous.
Neither Brad **nor** Jennifer has married again.
We use a plural verb after *both ... and ...* and a singular verb after *neither ... nor ...* .

3 Complete the sentences. Use *Both ... and ...* or *Neither ... nor ...* .

1 ...... *Seven* ...... *Fight Club* are Brad Pitt films.
2 ...... Gwyneth Paltrow ...... Tate Donovan was at the wedding.
3 ...... Antonio Banderas ...... Melanie Griffith is from England.

Writing task

4 Write a text about Antonio Banderas and Melanie Griffith. Use the information in the chart.

	Antonio	Melanie
Born?	Malaga 1960	New York 1957
Parents actors?	No	Yes, mother
First role?	1982	1975
Previous relationship?	Ana Laza	Don Johnson
Got married?	May 1996	

More practice? Workbook page 90

Learning Diary page 91

5 The world of work

UNIT FOCUS

- Jobs
- Suffixes: *-er*, *-or* and *-ist* for people
- Comparative and superlative adjectives
- *not as ... as*
- Expressing result: *so* and *such*
- At the post office
- Job application letter

VOCABULARY

Jobs

1 Match the jobs in the box with the pictures (1–12).

> architect cashier chef coach firefighter flight attendant lawyer plumber soldier surgeon tour guide vet

2 Listen, repeat and check your answers.

3 Complete the sentences. Use the jobs in exercise 1.

1. A ...... looks after sick animals.
2. A ...... repairs water pipes, bathrooms, etc.
3. An ...... designs buildings.
4. A ...... works in an army.
5. A ...... cooks food in a restaurant.
6. A ...... is a doctor who operates on people.
7. A ...... looks after passengers on a plane.
8. A ...... takes money from customers in shops or restaurants.
9. A ...... helps people with legal problems.
10. A ...... puts out fires.
11. A ...... helps sports people to train.
12. A ...... shows people round famous places.

4 Listen to the six recordings and identify the jobs.

More practice? Workbook page 92

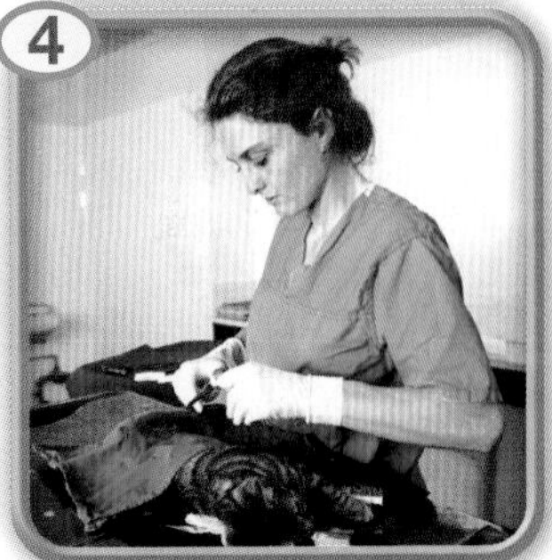

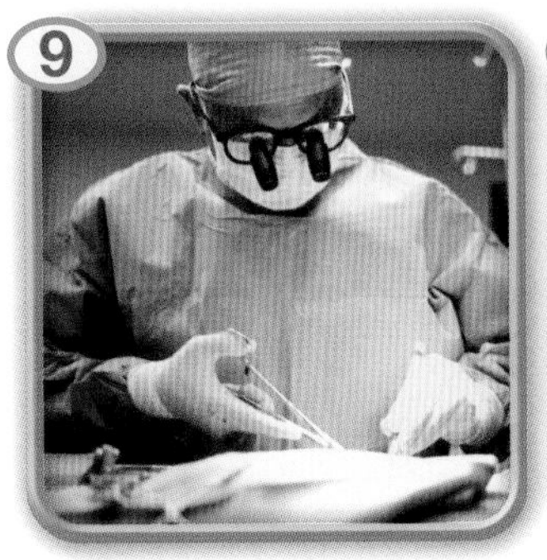

ABBY'S STORY
Good job!
1 I'm used to London now, but it's really different from Liverpool. London is more expensive, and the people are busier – they aren't as friendly as the people in Liverpool. There are exceptions, of course, like Rachel and Dan. Dan is the nicest boy I've met here. On Saturdays, he works in a bike shop near my house. Last Saturday, when I was walking past the shop, he saw me and asked about Victor, my brother. (He had an accident on his bike.)
How's Victor?
Dan
He's fine now. His bike needs a new wheel, though.
I can repair it here.
2 Dan came with me to get Victor's bike. Then he spent half an hour repairing it while I watched.
How much is the new wheel?
£40 – but because you're a friend, let's say £35. Don't tell my boss!
3 When I showed the bike to Victor, he was really pleased. But that night, I got an email from Dan
I lost my job at the bike repair shop. The boss found out! I offered to pay the extra five pounds, but it was too late. Never mind.
4 I felt so guilty. It was all my fault!

1 Read and listen to Abby's story. How much did Dan charge to repair Victor's bike?

a) £5 b) £35 c) £40

2 Put the events in the correct order.

a) Dan got Victor's bike from Abby's house.
b) Dan lost his job.
c) Dan saw Abby and asked about Victor.
d) Abby gave Dan £35 for the new wheel.
e) Abby watched Dan repairing the bike.
f) Dan offered to repair Victor's bike.
g) Abby got an email from Dan.

3 Answer the questions.

1 How does Abby think London is different from Liverpool?
2 Where does Dan work on Saturdays?
3 What happened to Abby's brother, Victor?
4 What's wrong with Victor's bike?
5 Why did Dan lose his job at the bike shop?

4 **REAL ENGLISH** Find equivalents for these sentences in the story.

1 London is familiar to me now.
2 The boss discovered what happened.
3 It doesn't matter.
4 I was responsible for everything.

5 **REAL ENGLISH** Rewrite the underlined words with expressions from exercise 4.

1 My new school is familiar to me now, but the first few weeks were difficult.
2 When his parents discovered that he was smoking, they were angry.
3 'I'd like to play tennis, but it's raining.' 'It doesn't matter.'
4 I didn't stop at the red light. I was responsible for everything.

What do you think?

Do you agree or disagree with these statements?

- Dan was wrong to charge Abby only £35 for the wheel.
- It was Abby's fault that Dan lost his job.

Vote YES or NO for each one and give your reasons.

Word help

Suffixes: *-er*, *-or* and *-ist* for people

Take note!

We use *-er*, *-or* and *-ist* to make the names of people who do a particular job or activity.

-er soldier plumber
-or director sailor visitor
-ist artist tourist journalist

6 Add *-er*, *-or* or *-ist*. Use a dictionary if necessary.

1 reception.... 5 firefight....
2 act.... 6 translat....
3 teach.... 7 wait....
4 chem.... 8 pian....

7 Complete the sentences. Use words from the *Take note!* box and exercise 6.

1 The hotel ...... answered the phone.
2 He speaks three languages, so he could become a ....
3 ...... ! Can I have another beer, please?
4 Lots of ...... visit La Recoleta every day.
5 Oh, no! There's water coming through the ceiling. Phone the ...... !
6 'Who's your favourite ......?' 'Adam Brody.'
7 The ...... interviewed the actors.

More practice? Workbook page 92

Pronunciation Word stress and the weak vowel

1 Listen and repeat. Pay attention to the stressed syllable (•) and the weak vowel (•).

A Stress on 1st syllable	plumber better
B Stress on 2nd syllable	address arrive

2 Listen and mark the stressed syllable (•) and the weak vowel (•).

1 soldier 3 about 5 further
2 correct 4 longer 6 around

Comparative and superlative adjectives

1 **Study the sentences and complete the rules.**

> Hanif is **taller than** Dan.
> London is **more expensive than** Liverpool.
> Dan is **the nicest** boy I've met.
> Rachel is **the most intelligent** girl in the class.

Short adjectives

1 The comparative form ends in ....
2 The superlative form ends in ....

Long adjectives

3 The comparative form is ...... + adjective.
4 The superlative form is ...... + adjective.

2 **Write the comparative and superlative forms.**

1 sad
2 boring
3 artistic
4 thin
5 large
6 trendy
7 early
8 late
9 exciting
10 embarrassing

Watch out!

We use *than* when we compare two people or things.
Ben is shorter ~~that~~ Nigel. ✗
Ben is shorter **than** Nigel. ✓

3 **Complete the sentences with the comparative form and *than*. Then say if you agree or disagree.**

1 Lawyers are usually ...... (rich) chefs.
2 Being a firefighter is ...... (dangerous) being a soldier.
3 A vet's job is ...... (easy) an architect's job.
4 For a football team, a great coach is ...... (important) a great player.
5 A flight attendant's job is ...... (interesting) a tour guide's job.
6 A chef's life ...... (good) a plumber's life.

Take note!

Some adjectives are irregular.
good – better – the best
bad – worse – the worst
far – further – the furthest

4 **Give your opinions. Use the superlative form.**

1 – I think the best singer in the world is ...
1 (good) singer / in the world
2 (dangerous) job / in the world
3 (interesting) school subject
4 (bad) song / in the world
5 (cold) town / in Argentina
6 (attractive) person / in the world

5 **Complete the interview. Use the comparative or superlative form of the adjectives in the box.**

big close exciting far interested ~~interesting~~ successful tiring

Do you travel with your job?
Yes, I do. It's probably the most interesting thing about my job. However, it's also the (**1**) .... thing. The competitions take place all over the world and I spend a lot of time flying. The (**2**) ...... one is in Australia, about 17,000 kilometres away!

Do you earn a lot of money?
No, I don't. Last year was my (**3**) ...... year and I earned about £20,000. The prizes for men are (**4**) .... That's because TV companies are (**5**) ...... in the men's sport.

What are the best things about your job?
I love the people – the other surfers. We're (**6**) ...... than most families! And of course, I love surfing. It's the (**7**) ...... sport in the world!

More practice? Workbook pages 93–94

Dialogue

1 Read and listen. Did Hanif send the parcel by airmail or by surface mail?

At the post office

Clerk	Next, please.
Hanif	Hello. Can I send this parcel to Pakistan, please?
Clerk	Sure. Put it on the scales … By airmail or surface mail?
Hanif	Um, how much is airmail?
Clerk	£9.10. It's cheaper by surface mail – £3.52 – but it takes longer.
Hanif	OK, I'll send it by airmail. Can I have a stamp for this letter, too?
Clerk	First class or second class?
Hanif	First class.
Clerk	That's £9.46 altogether, please. Thank you. Here's your change.
Hanif	Thanks. Bye.
Clerk	Thank you. Goodbye.

2 **REAL ENGLISH** Listen and repeat these expressions. What do they mean?

1 Next, please.
2 by airmail
3 altogether
4 Here's your change.

3 Practise reading the dialogue.

4 Write your own dialogue. Choose different countries and prices.

A: Next, please.
B: Hello. Can I send this parcel to … , please?

5 Act out your dialogue.

More practice? Workbook page 94

Listening

6 Listen. What do the girl and boy want to do? Complete the chart.

	Gina	Ben
send a postcard		
send letters to Spain		
apply for a passport		

7 Listen again. Are the sentences true or false? Correct the false ones.

1 Gina has got four letters to post.
2 One letter costs 40p and three cost 57p.
3 Gina gives the clerk £10.
4 The post box is outside the post office.
5 Ben is going abroad soon.
6 Ben has to send the form to the passport office in the USA.
7 The stamp costs 35p.

GRAMMAR 2

not as … as

Take note!

We can use *not as* + adjective + *as* to compare two people or things.
James **isn't as** tall **as** Carlos.
= Carlos is taller than James.

1 Compare the footballers. Use *not as … as* and the adjectives in the box.

expensive fast heavy ~~old~~ rich short tall young

Wayne Rooney isn't as old as Thierry Henry.

	Thierry Henry	Wayne Rooney
Date of birth	17.8.77	24.10.85
Height	1m 85cm	1m 80cm
Speed	➡	➡
Salary	£40,000 a week	£50,000 a week
Weight	83 kg	77 kg
Transfer value	about £50 million	about £60 million

Communicate!

Write sentences about famous people.
Kylie Minogue isn't as tall as Madonna.

Expressing result: *so* and *such*

2 Study the information and complete the rules.

Take note!

We use *so* and *such* to make the meaning of an adjective stronger.
Rachel passed all her exams. She's **so** intelligent!
I really like Dan. He's **such** a nice boy.

We can use *so* and *such* with *that* to talk about result.
Abby felt **so** guilty **that** she couldn't sleep.
Abby had **such** a strange feeling about Victor **that** she knew something was wrong.

1 We use …… with an adjective without a noun.
2 We use …… with an adjective and a noun.

3 Join the sentences using *so … that* or *such … that*.

It was a really nice day. We decided to go to the beach.
It was such a nice day that we decided to go to the beach.
He's really intelligent. He never fails an exam.
He's so intelligent that he never fails an exam.

1 It's a really good film. I want to see it again.
2 She was really excited. She couldn't sleep.
3 It was a really boring concert. She left early.
4 It was really windy. We couldn't play tennis.
5 It was a really big pizza. I couldn't finish it.
6 We were really tired. We had to go to bed.
7 It was a really difficult exam. Only three people passed.
8 It was a really nice holiday. We want to go back there next year.
9 I was really worried. I couldn't sleep.

More practice? Workbook pages 93–94

1 Are these sentences true or false for you?

1. I know what I want to do when I leave school.
2. I haven't thought very much about jobs.
3. I'd like my favourite hobby or interest to become my job.

2 Read the text. Would you like to have any of the three jobs? Give reasons.

Claire

At the age of sixteen, most people have just started to think about the kind of job they might do when they're older. A few people have gone further than that – they've already started work. Here are three sixteen-year-olds who are already serious about their career.

Shanaze Reade: BMX champion

Shanaze Reade is officially the best BMX rider in the world for her age. She's very serious about the sport. She didn't really celebrate her sixteenth birthday because she was preparing for the British BMX Championships at the time, and that was more important. Jamie Staff, a former BMX champion, says: 'I'm sure she'll be the sport's fastest woman.'

Shanaze says: 'My long-term goal is to be Olympic champion.'

Rupert Grint: actor

At the age of eleven, Rupert didn't have much experience of acting. However, he went to the auditions for the first *Harry Potter* film and got one of the biggest roles: Harry's friend, Ron Weasley.

According to the film's producer, Rupert is 'a natural comedian' and has 'great instinct and talent'. Rupert says: 'I hope to carry on playing Ron and to get the opportunity to do more comedy.'

Rupert was working on the latest *Harry Potter* film at the time of his sixteenth birthday.

Claire Calvert: ballet dancer

Claire has been a student at the Royal Ballet School in London since the age of eleven. Now sixteen, she is one of the most promising dancers at the school and has already worked with two professional ballet companies.

For Claire, the best thing about being sixteen is that now she doesn't have to live at the school – she can share a flat with her friends. The worst thing is that her body is changing as she gets older. 'That's harder as a dancer,' she says, 'because your body is in the spotlight.' Claire spent her sixteenth birthday at school with her friends.

3 Read the text again. Answer the questions.

1. What was Shanaze doing on her sixteenth birthday?
2. What is Shanaze's long-term goal?
3. How old was Rupert when he got the role of Ron Weasley?
4. What would Rupert like to do in in the future?
5. Where does Claire study ballet?
6. Where does Claire live now that she's sixteen?

4 WORD CHECK Find the words (1–8) in the text and match them to the meanings (a–h).

1 career (line 6)
2 former (line 13)
3 long-term (line 15)
4 roles (line 21)
5 carry on (line 24)
6 latest (line 26)
7 promising (line 31)
8 in the spotlight (line 39)

a) previous; from the past
b) parts (in a film)
c) with a good future
d) job; professional life
e) not immediate or soon
f) continue
g) in public view
h) most recent

WRITING

Model text A formal letter

1 Read the advertisement and the letter.

Part-time staff

Better Burgers

We have vacancies for cashiers and kitchen staff to help in one of the busiest restaurants in town on Saturdays between 9.00 and 18.00. Applicants should be over 14 years old, hard-working and enthusiastic. Pay: £6 an hour.

Please write to:
Ms Sarah Harman, Better Burgers, 194 High St, Oxford OX1 9WS

87 Whitehouse Rd
Oxford OX5 5JK

10th March 2006

Ms S. Harman
Better Burgers
194 High St
Oxford OX1 9WS

Dear Ms Harman,
I saw your advertisement for part-time staff in the local paper and I am writing to apply for a job as a cashier in your restaurant in Oxford.

I am 16 years old and I am a student at St Mary's School. I am friendly, hard-working and good at maths. My teachers always say that I am one of the most responsible people in my class. I've worked as a waitress in a café and I have served customers in a shop, so I am used to working with people.

At the moment, I am working in a newsagent's. It's very small and quiet, so I am looking for a more interesting job in a busier place. The earliest date that I could start working at Better Burgers is Saturday 1st April.

I am sending you my photo, and I look forward to hearing from you.

Yours sincerely,

Rebecca Smith

Rebecca Smith

2 Answer the questions.

1 Where did Rebecca see the advertisement?
2 Which job is she applying for?
3 What three jobs has she had?
4 Why does she want to change jobs?
5 What's the earliest date she could start working?

Job application letter

3 Answer the questions.

1 Where does Rebecca write her address?
2 Where is the date?
3 Where is Better Burgers' address?
4 How does Rebecca start the letter?
5 How does she finish it?

Writing task

4 Write a letter of application for this job.

Part-time staff

STARLIGHT CAFÉ

We have vacancies for waiters or waitresses and kitchen helpers in our café on Fridays between 18.00 and 22.00. Applicants should be 16 or over, smart and hard-working. Pay: £7 an hour.

Please write to:
Peter Bridges, Starlight Café, 54 Market St, Oxford OX4 3SD

Paragraph 1
I saw ... and I'm writing ...
Paragraph 2
I am ... and I'm a student at ...
I'm ... (Describe your character)
I've worked ... (What jobs have you done?)
Paragraph 3
At the moment, ... (Where are you working now?) I could start ...
Paragraph 4
I'm sending ... and I look forward ...

More practice? Workbook page 95

Learning Diary page 96

Revision: Units 4–5

VOCABULARY

Relationships and dating

1 **Complete the phrases. Use the correct order, from the beginning to the end of a relationship.**

an argument in love married
somebody somebody somebody out
up up

1 meet …… 4 fall …… 7 make ……
2 fancy …… 5 have …… 8 get ……
3 ask …… 6 split ……

Noun endings: *-ion* and *-ment*

2 **Form nouns from these verbs by adding *-ion* or *-ment*.**

1 arrange 5 entertain
2 collect 6 invent
3 discuss 7 announce
4 embarrass 8 translate

Jobs

3 **Complete the jobs using *a*, *e*, *i*, *o*, *u* and *y*.**

1 c_sh__r (picture _)
2 c__ch (picture _)
3 l_w__r (picture _)
4 s_ld__r (picture _)
5 s_rg__n (picture _)
6 t__r g__d_ (picture _)

Suffixes: *-er*, *-or* and *-ist* for people

4 **Complete the words. Use *-er*, *-or* or *-ist*.**

1 wait….. 4 act….. 7 pian…..
2 chem….. 5 soldi….. 8 direct…..
3 teach….. 6 tour….. 9 translat…..

GRAMMAR

Present perfect interrogative

1 **What have they done today? Write questions and answers using the present perfect.**

	pizza	homework	phone
Liz	✗	✔	✔
Joe	✔	✗	✔
Erica	✔	✗	✗
Terry	✗	✔	✔

Liz / eat / a pizza
Has Liz eaten a pizza?
No, she hasn't.

1 Joe and Erica / eat / a pizza?
2 Joe and Erica / do / their homework?
3 Terry / do / his homework?
4 Liz and Joe / phone / their friends?
5 Erica / phone / her friend?

2 **Write questions in the present perfect and match them with the answers (a–e).**

1 where / you / put / my bag?
2 what / you / eat / today?
3 why / you / get up / so early?
4 how many people / you / invite to your party?
5 how often / you / visit / London?

a) Some cereal and a banana.
b) Twelve.
c) In the kitchen.
d) Three times.
e) Because I'm going on holiday.

for and *since*

3 **Complete the sentences with *for* and *since*.**

1 I've lived in England …… 1992.
2 She's been married …… two years.
3 He's played tennis …… the age of four.
4 They've had a dog …… Christmas.
5 I've been a Chelsea fan …… ten years.
6 Sue hasn't eaten any crisps …… Monday.

How long ...?

4 Read the answers. Then write questions with *How long ...?*

How long has she been a student?
She's been a student for three years.

1 He's had a headache for two hours.
2 She's played the guitar since the age of five.
3 They've wanted a new car for years.
4 He's lived in that house since 1949.
5 They've been in the park since lunchtime.

Past simple and present perfect

5 Complete the sentences. Use the past simple or present perfect.

1 My brother ...... (get) engaged last December.
2 ...... (you / ever / fall) in love?
3 'When's Mike arriving?' 'He ...... (already / arrive).'
4 We ...... (meet) six months ago.
5 ...... (you / finish) your homework yet?
6 I ...... (never / have) an argument with my boyfriend.
7 I ...... (get up) at eight o'clock this morning.

Comparative and superlative adjectives

6 Look at the cars and write sentences. Use the comparative form of the adjective and *than*.

The red car (cheap) ...
The red car is cheaper than the blue car.

1 The yellow car (big) ...
2 The yellow car (old) ...
3 The red car (expensive) ...
4 The yellow car (new) ...
5 The yellow car (small) ...

7 Write sentences about the cars. Use the superlative form of the adjective.

1 - The blue car is the biggest.

1	big	5	cheap
2	small	6	expensive
3	new	7	clean
4	old	8	dirty

not as ... as

8 Rewrite the sentences. Use *not as ... as* and an adjective with the opposite meaning.

Jack is younger than Megan.
Jack isn't as old as Megan.

1 Buenos Aires is cheaper than Tokyo.
2 The trumpet is easier to play than the piano.
3 Helen's hair is longer than Lisa's hair.
4 The station is nearer than the airport.
5 China is smaller than Russia.
6 Sue is shorter than Liam.

Expressing result: *so* and *such*

9 Complete the sentences. Use *so* or *such*.

1 He's got ...... a boring job!
2 The bus was ...... slow that she was late for work.
3 She had ...... a bad headache that she went to see the doctor.
4 Stop doing that! You're ...... annoying!
5 It was ...... an easy exam that I got 99%.
6 I love Robbie Williams. He's got ...... a beautiful voice.
7 It was ...... cold that we couldn't go out.
8 I was ...... tired that I fell asleep on the sofa.

Build up: Units 1–5

1 **Complete the text. Choose the correct words.**

1 a) 'm trying b) try
2 a) doing b) to do
3 a) did it take b) took it
4 a) was going b) used to go
5 a) was having b) had
6 a) was sitting b) sat
7 a) seen b) saw
8 a) 've received b) received
9 a) haven't spoken b) didn't speak
10 a) more friendly b) friendlier
11 a) than b) that
12 a) more boring b) most boring
13 a) so b) such
14 a) I haven't finished b) I didn't finish
15 a) I meet b) I'm meeting

Dear Daisy

It's Saturday afternoon and I **(1)** ...... *to finish my history homework before the evening. I don't mind* **(2)** ...... *homework in the afternoon, but evenings are different. I'm meeting some friends at seven o'clock.*

I really liked that photo of you at the beach. Who **(3)** ......? *I* **(4)** ...... *there every Sunday morning, so it brought back lots of memories. I met Max there for the first time. Do you remember? I* **(5)** ...... *a cola after swimming when he* **(6)** ...... *down at my table.*

Have you **(7)** ...... *Max recently? I* **(8)** ...... *an email from him a few days ago, but I* **(9)** ...... *to him since last week.*

I'm making lots of new friends here. I think the people in Manchester are **(10)** ...... **(11)** ...... *the people in London. (Not including you, of course!) Last night, I went out with some friends and we watched the* **(12)** ...... *film in the world. In fact, I was* **(13)** ...... *bored that I fell asleep in the cinema!*

Oh no, I've just noticed the time – it's nearly seven o'clock. **(14)** ...... *my homework! I have to go now.* **(15)** ...... *my friends in five minutes.*

Love,

Hannah

2 **Answer the questions.**

1 What is Hannah trying to finish?
2 When is she meeting her friends?
3 What was Hannah doing the first time she met Max?
4 Has she spoken to Max this week?
5 What does Hannah think of the people in Manchester?
6 What did she think of the film that she saw last night?

3 **Correct the mistakes.**

My brother **is believing** in a sixth sense. ✗
My brother believes in a sixth sense. ✓

1 We can't play tennis. It **rains**. ✗
2 I **did** my homework when the telephone rang. ✗
3 I **used to went** to my local primary school. ✗
4 I'm not as tall **that** my brother. ✗
5 We've **seen just** that film. ✗
6 I haven't been to the beach **for** last summer ✗
7 They got married **ago two years**. ✗
8 My brother is **more nice** than my sister. ✗
9 She's the most intelligent girl **of** the class. ✗
10 How long has she been a student **since.** ✗

Irregular verbs

base form	past simple	past participle
be	was / were	been
become	became	become
begin	began	begun
bite	bit	bitten
break	broke	broken
bring	brought	brought
build	built	built
burn	burned, burnt	burned, burnt
buy	bought	bought
catch	caught	caught
choose	chose	chosen
come	came	come
cost	cost	cost
cut	cut	cut
do	did	done
draw	drew	drawn
dream	dreamt	dreamt
drink	drank	drunk
drive	drove	driven
eat	ate	eaten
fall	fell	fallen
feed	fed	fed
feel	felt	felt
fight	fought	fought
find	found	found
fly	flew	flown
forget	forgot	forgotten
freeze	froze	frozen
get	got	got
give	gave	given
go	went	been / gone
grow	grew	grown
have	had	had
hear	heard	heard
hit	hit	hit
hold	held	held
hurt	hurt	hurt
keep	kept	kept

base form	past simple	past participle
know	knew	known
learn	learnt, learned	learnt, learned
leave	left	left
lend	lent	lent
let	let	let
lose	lost	lost
make	made	made
meet	met	met
pay	paid	paid
put	put	put
read	read	read
ride	rode	ridden
ring	rang	rung
run	ran	run
say	said	said
see	saw	seen
sell	sold	sold
send	sent	sent
shine	shone	shone
shut	shut	shut
sing	sang	sung
sit	sat	sat
sleep	slept	slept
speak	spoke	spoken
spend	spend	spent
stand	stood	stood
steal	stole	stolen
swim	swam	swum
swing	swung	swung
take	took	taken
teach	taught	taught
tell	told	told
think	thought	thought
throw	threw	thrown
wake	woke	woken
wear	wore	worn
win	won	won
write	wrote	written

TEEN REPORTS

Teen voices

1 **Read the sentences about Britain. Do you think it's the same in your own country?**

1 Britain is a multi-cultural society.
2 Immigrants sometimes face discrimination in Britain.
3 More than three-quarters of teenagers (77%) have got friends of different races.

2 **Read the report. Find similarities and differences between Britain and your own country.**

Multi-cultural Britain

Britain has always been a multi-cultural society. For thousands of years, different people have made Britain their home. Celts, Romans, Saxons, Vikings and Normans all invaded Britain between 500 BC and 1100 AD. However, smaller groups have continued to arrive. In the middle of the nineteenth century hundreds of thousands of Irish people emigrated to Britain, and thousands of people from Eastern Europe came here in the first half of the twentieth century. These people were escaping from terrible conditions in their own countries: in Ireland it was famine; in Eastern Europe it was the result of war.

Quick fact

Nearly a third of immigrants (30%) said they experienced discrimination at school.

Other people came for economic reasons: in the 1950s and 1960s, there weren't enough workers in Britain, so people from British colonies and former colonies in the Caribbean and Asia came to work here. The most recent arrivals in Britain are refugees who have escaped from war and political persecution in countries like Afghanistan, Yugoslavia and Iraq. But life isn't always easy when they arrive. They have to build a new life in a new country. Many can't speak English so it can be difficult to find work or understand what is happening at school. Sometimes they face discrimination because people don't always understand who they are and why they have come.

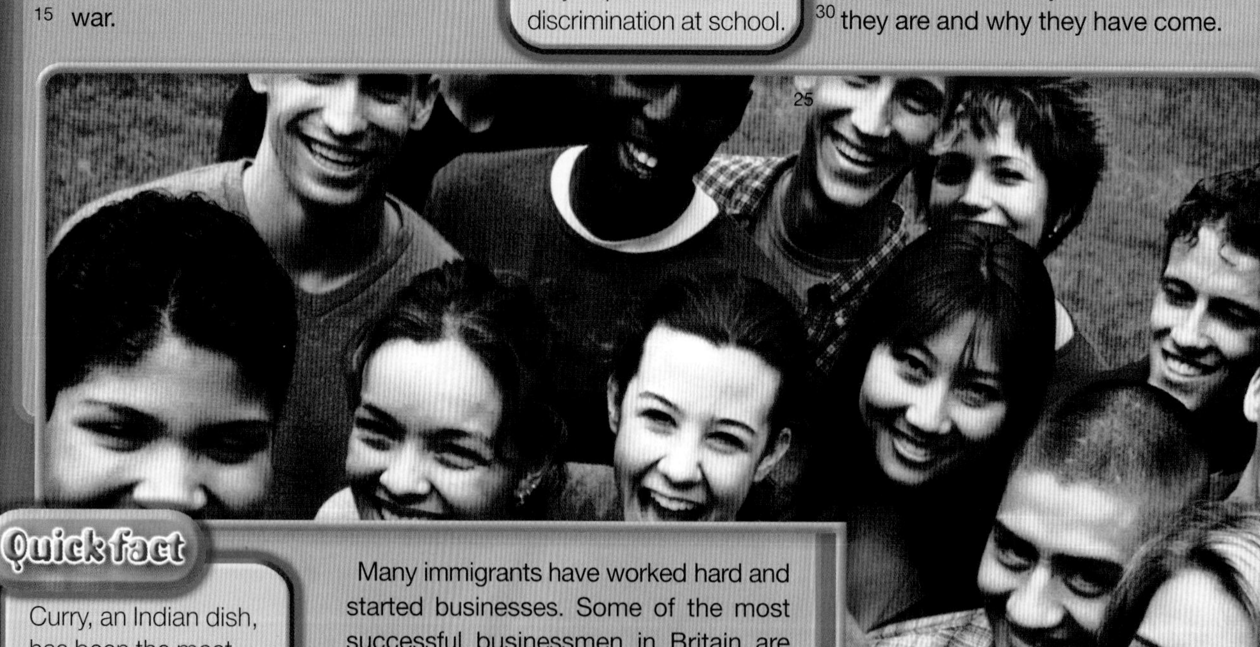

Quick fact

Curry, an Indian dish, has been the most popular food in Britain for more than 10 years.

Many immigrants have worked hard and started businesses. Some of the most successful businessmen in Britain are Asian. Immigrants have also had an important cultural influence on life in Britain, especially in the areas of music, fashion and food. For example, West Indians started the Notting Hill Carnival in London in 1960, and now it's the biggest street festival in Europe. There are Chinese and Indian restaurants in almost every town in Britain. And reggae and rap music form the Caribbean have heavily influenced British pop music. Britain is a richer and more interesting country because of its immigrants.

3 **Answer the questions.**

1 Which peoples invaded Britain between 500 BC and 1000 AD?
2 Why did Irish people and Eastern European people come to Britain in the nineteenth and twentieth centuries?
3 Where did immigrants come from in the 1950s and 1960s?
4 Why have people arrived from countries like Afghanistan, Yugoslavia and Iraq?
5 Who started the Notting Hill Carnival?
6 What is the most popular dish in Britain, and where does it come from?

4 **WORD CHECK** **Find these words and phrases in the text. Then use them to complete the definitions.**

colonies discrimination emigrate immigrants multi-cultural persecution refugees

1 Racial ...... is treating people differently because they are a different colour.
2 ...... are people who have moved permanently to another country.
3 Political ...... is treating people in a cruel way because they have different political beliefs.
4 ...... are countries which are part of another country's empire.
5 If you ...... to another country, you go and live there permanently.
6 A ...... place is a place where people from different countries and cultures live together.
7 .... are people who have travelled abroad to escape from war or persecution in their own country.

5 **Match the words to make phrases. Find examples of the phrases in the text.**

1 face
2 escape from
3 invade
4 build
5 have

a) a country
b) an influence
c) persecution
d) discrimination
e) a new life

6 **Listen and match the four teenagers with the places in the box. Who doesn't speak two languages?**

Belfast Bradford Glasgow London

1 Julie

2 Goran

3 Badal

4 Lin

7 **Listen again. Choose the correct answers.**

1 Where does Julie's family originally come from?
a) England b) Jamaica
2 Where was Julie born?
a) England b) Jamaica
3 What job did Goran's dad use to do?
a) taxi driver b) businessman
4 What job does Goran's mum do?
a) taxi driver b) cleaner
5 How many people live in Badal's house?
a) 6 b) 7
6 How many Chinese people live in Northern Ireland?
a) 8,000 b) 80,000

8 **Discuss these questions with the class.**

1 What problems do immigrants from other countries sometimes face?
2 What can be done to minimise these problems?
3 How do immigrants affect the culture of the place where they settle?

Teen USA

1 **In pairs, think of three examples of:**

1. styles of music from the USA
2. American food
3. TV programmes made in the USA
4. clothes from the USA

2 **Read the report. Can you find any more examples to add to your list in exercise 1?**

American culture

Quick fact

Caroline Davidson, a university student, designed the logo for Nike in 1971. She was paid $35.

The USA is sometimes called the 'Land of Opportunity'. Americans are famous for having enthusiasm for new ideas. In any country in Europe you will find shopping malls, multi-screen cinemas, theme parks – all these first appeared in the USA. In the entertainment and leisure industries America has had a particularly strong influence, and ideas and products from the USA have spread all around the world …

Films and TV

Hollywood produces about 600 films a year. Although many countries have their own film industries and make excellent films, most of the films in cinemas around the world are American. In addition, television channels in many countries are full of American TV shows like *The O.C.*, *Charmed* and *ER*. A lot of people around the world copy the American way of life that they see in these films and TV programmes.

Music

The USA has had a bigger influence on popular music than any other country. Many styles of music e.g. jazz, blues, soul music and hip-hop, originated in black American culture. Blues, for example, came from the religious songs that were sung by African slaves in the USA. A century later, hip-hop was a form of expression for young black Americans living in big cities.

Fashion

Many styles of casual clothes started in the USA. Since the 1950s, jeans and T-shirts have become the most popular clothes in the world. Today, baseball caps are worn in countries where nobody plays baseball. Sports clothes made by American companies such as Nike are worn by millions of young people all around the world.

Quick fact

McDonald's has 27,000 restaurants in 119 different countries. They serve 43 million customers a day.

Food

The expression 'Time is money' originated in the USA. Americans are famous for doing things fast and wanting things fast. And that's probably why they invented fast food! Hot dogs and hamburgers originated in the USA, and today millions of people around the world use American-style fast food restaurants every day.

3 Answer the questions.

1 According to the text, what do people sometimes call the USA?
2 How many films are made in Hollywood every year?
3 Which style of music came from religious songs?
4 Who designed the Nike logo?
5 What famous American expression is quoted in the text?
6 In how many countries are there McDonald's restaurants?

4 **WORD CHECK** Match the words (1–5) with the definitions (a–e).

1 produce a) 100 years
2 originated b) company symbol
3 century c) make
4 logo d) started
5 customer e) person who buys something

5 Listen to four teenagers talking about the influence of American culture. Which two really like US culture?

1 Sam

2 Lou

3 Dean

4 Beth

6 Listen again. Which teenagers talk about the subjects in the chart? What is their opinion of them: positive or negative? Copy and complete the chart.

P = Positive **N** = Negative

	Sam	Lou	Dean	Beth
1 fast food	P			
2 TV programmes				
3 clothes				
4 music				
5 films				
6 shopping malls				
7 multi-screen cinemas				

7 Listen again. Choose the correct answer.

1 Sam eats fast food ...... times a week.
a) 2 or 3 b) 3 or 4 c) 5 or 6
2 Sam mentions *South Park* and ....
a) *Charmed* b) *ER*
c) *The Simpsons*
3 Lou loves wearing jeans and ....
a) baseball caps b) T-shirts
c) baggy tops
4 Dean thinks that people who don't like fast food ....
a) are wrong b) are right
c) shouldn't eat it
5 Dean mentions ...... different styles of popular music.
a) 2 b) 3 c) 4
6 Beth thinks the worst American TV programmes are the ....
a) comedies b) police dramas
c) documentaries

8 Work in pairs or groups. Talk about what are some of the positive and negative effects of American culture on your country.

I think American films are really good and ...

The only good thing about American culture is ...

Teen rights

1 **Read the sentences. Do you agree or disagree?**

1 Parents should have complete control over their children's lives until they are 18.
2 Adults should listen to children's opinions more often.

2 **Complete the UN Convention on the Rights of the Child. Use the words and phrases in the box.**

opinions and information a healthy life protection from dangerous work a family equality education an identity

3 **Read the UN convention on the Rights of the Child. Which three rights do you think are the most important? Give reasons?**

The UN Convention on the Rights of the Child

1 The right to ......
The right to a name and a nationality, and the right to know who your parents are.

2 The right to ......
The right to live with your parents, or if this isn't possible, the right to have special protection.

3 The right to ......
The right to health, and the right to see a doctor.

4 The right to ......
The right to believe what you want, to express opinions, to meet friends, and the right to get information about the world.

5 The right to ......
The right to primary and secondary education.

6 The right to ......
The right not to do dangerous work, and the right to rest and to play.

7 The right to ......
Equal rights for boys and girls and ethnic minorities, and the right to your own culture, religion and language.

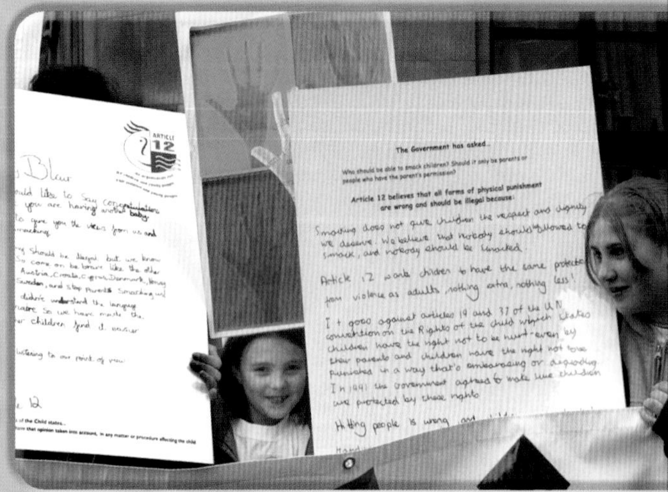

Article 12

Article 12 is a children's rights organisation in the UK. It is named after Article 12 of the UN Convention on the Rights of the Child, which says: *Whenever an adult makes a decision that will affect you in any way, you have the right to give your opinion and be taken seriously*.

Twenty-four young people work for *Article 12* in the UK. They meet every six weeks in London. Anyone under 18 can join and there are now over 500 members.

Article 12 wants every young person to know their rights under the UN convention, and it encourages them to express their opinions and get involved in politics. In its most recent campaign, it organised a big demonstration in London against smacking. Members of *Article 12* delivered a letter to the British Prime Minister, asking the British government to make smacking illegal.

Quick fact

There are only two countries that haven't ratified the convention: the USA and Somalia. (*ratify* = to make an agreement)

4 Read about *Article 12*. Answer the questions.

1 What is *Article 12*?
2 Why is it called *Article 12*?
3 How many people work for *Article 12* and how often do they meet?
4 How many members are there in the organisation?
5 What did it do in its most recent campaign?

5 **WORD CHECK** Find words in the two texts that mean:

1 well; not ill
2 that may hurt you
3 relax and not do anything
4 small groups of people from a different race or culture
5 at any time when
6 hitting a child with a flat hand

6 Work with a partner. Look at the facts box. At what age can you do these things in your country?

FACTS

In the UK young people can …

1 get a part-time job when they're 13.
2 buy cigarettes when they're 16.
3 get married when they're 16 (but only with their parents' permission).
4 leave school when they're 16.
5 join the army when they're 16.
6 drive a car when they're 17.
7 drink alcohol in a bar when they're 18.
8 vote when they're 18.

7 Listen to three teenagers. Which facts in exercise 6 do the speakers mention?

1 Martin

2 Tina

3 Andrew

1 Martin: 4, …
2 Tina:
3 Andrew:

8 Listen again. True or false? Correct the false sentences.

1 Martin thinks the different ages don't make sense.
2 Martin thinks young people should be able to do all these things when they are 18.
3 Tina thinks that parents should decide when their children should get married.
4 Tina thinks young people should wait until they are 21 before getting married.
5 In Andrew's opinion, 16 year-olds should be able to buy cigarettes and smoke.
6 Andrew thinks that if he's old enough to die for his country, he's old enough to vote.

9 Work with a partner. Would you change the ages at which you can smoke, vote, get married, etc.? Give reasons.

I don't think young people should …

I think we should be allowed to …

Teen spending

1 **In pairs, ask and answer the questions.**

1 Do you get pocket money?
2 What do you usually spend it on?

2 **Read the report. Match the headings (1–3) with the sections (A–C).**

1 What do they spend it on?
2 The pressure to spend
3 Where do teenagers get their money?

Young people with money to spend

- In the UK, 67% of teenagers receive regular pocket money.
- On average, teenagers receive £10 a week.
- On average, boys get £1 more pocket money per week than girls. (5)
- 56% are given the money by their parents and 14% by their grandparents.
- 15% have to earn their pocket money by doing housework.
- Some teenagers have jobs. The most popular job for girls is babysitting, and the most popular job for boys is doing a paper round. (10)

A lot of young people in the UK spend money on clothes, music and videos, going out and making mobile phone calls. Books are at the bottom of the list! Girls spend a lot more than boys on clothes and cosmetics. Boys spend (15) more than girls on computer games and snacks and drinks.

	All teenagers £	Boys £	Girls £
Clothes/sportswear	3.68	2.47	3.92
CDs/videos	2.79	2.73	2.89
Going out	2.37	2.10	2.64
Savings	2.34	2.66	1.99
Mobile phone	1.75	1.71	1.79
Snacks/drinks	1.66	1.96	1.32
Gifts	1.61	1.41	1.81
Computer games	1.56	2.56	0.50
Holidays	0.99	0.93	1.04
Magazines	0.98	0.98	0.98
Cosmetics	0.88	0.33	1.48
Books	0.55	0.54	0.57

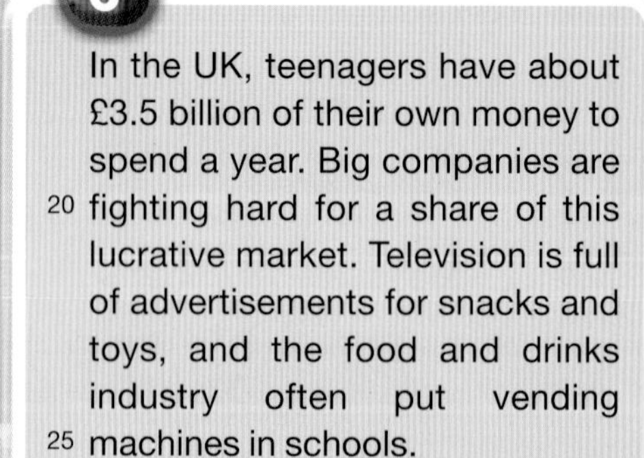

C

In the UK, teenagers have about £3.5 billion of their own money to spend a year. Big companies are (20) fighting hard for a share of this lucrative market. Television is full of advertisements for snacks and toys, and the food and drinks industry often put vending (25) machines in schools.

However, companies like IBM and Kellogg are trying to help schools as well as promote their products to the students. For (30) example, the 'Computers for Schools' project, run by the supermarket, Tesco, has given 50,000 computers to schools.

3 **True or false? Correct the false sentences.**

1. About two thirds of teenagers get regular pocket money.
2. On average, girls get more than boys.
3. Teenagers spend the most on mobile phone calls.
4. They spend more on books than on magazines.
5. Teenagers have over £5 billion a year to spend.
6. Some companies have helped schools by providing equipment.

4 **WORD CHECK** **Find words in section C that mean:**

1. 1,000,000,000
2. making a lot of money
3. food that you eat quickly between meals
4. a machine from which you can buy drinks, sweets, crisps, etc.
5. to advertise

5 **Listen. What do these four teenagers spend their money on? Copy and complete the chart.**

1 Claire

2 Kevin

3 Suzanne

4 Oliver

	Claire	Kevin	Suzanne	Oliver
CDs				
clothes				
computer games				
cosmetics				
going out	✓			
magazines				
mobile phone				
snacks				

6 **Listen again. Answer the questions.**

1. Where does Claire work, and how much does she earn?
2. How much does Claire spend on cosmetics?
3. How often does Kevin get money from his parents?
4. How much does Kevin get?
5. Why doesn't Kevin buy CDs?
6. How does Suzanne earn money?
7. What's Suzanne going to do after her exams?
8. How many CDs does Oliver buy every month?
9. Where does Oliver buy snacks?

7 **In pairs, discuss these statements. Do you agree or disagree?**

1. It's good for teenagers to have their own money. They learn to become more independent.
2. Teenagers should earn pocket money by helping out at home.
3. Teenagers shouldn't have part-time jobs. They should concentrate on education.
4. Teenagers shouldn't get more than £10 a week pocket money.

OXFORD
UNIVERSITY PRESS
Great Clarendon Street, Oxford OX2 6DP
Oxford University Press is a department of the University of Oxford.
It furthers the University's objective of excellence in research, scholarship,
and education by publishing worldwide in
Oxford New York
Auckland Cape Town Dar es Salaam Hong Kong Karachi
Kuala Lumpur Madrid Melbourne Mexico City Nairobi
New Delhi Shanghai Taipei Toronto
With offices in
Argentina Austria Brazil Chile Czech Republic France Greece
Guatemala Hungary Italy Japan Poland Portugal Singapore
South Korea Switzerland Thailand Turkey Ukraine Vietnam
OXFORD and OXFORD ENGLISH are registered trade marks of
Oxford University Press in the UK and in certain other countries

First published 2008
2012 2011 2010 2009 2008
10 9 8 7 6 5 4 3 2 1

ISBN: 978 0 19 415328 7

Printed in China

ACKNOWLEDGEMENTS

Illustrations supplied by: Mona Daly/Mendola Art pp. 22 (ex 8), 30 (ex 1), 35, 37, 53, 54; Bruno Drummond p. 12; Jonathan Edwards pp. 11, 25; Spike Gerrell pp. 68, 72, 82; Sophie Joyce/New Division pp. 9, 33; Kveta/Three in a Box pp. 77, 87; David Oakley/Arnos Design p. 2 (map); Gavin Reece/New Division p. 40; Dylan Teague pp. 17, 22 (ex 9); Scott Thigpen/Three in a Box pp. 30 (ex 3), 35, 42.

Main story photoshoot and Everyday English: Chris King.

We would also like to thank the following for their permission to reproduce photographs: Action Plus pp. 14, 68; Alamy pp. 12, 28, 32 (both), 45 (1, 3, 7, 8, 10, 11), 48, 52, 84; British Cycling Magazine p. 51 (Reade); Chris Nash p. 51 (Claire Calvert); Corbis pp. 16, 24, 35 (girl in shades); Empics pp. 15 (Ronaldo), 85 (ex 6); Getty Images pp. 9 (b, e, f), 25 (1, 2, 3, 5), 31, 33, 36 (boy), 40, 42, 43 (1), 45 (2, 5, 9, 12), 50 (Rooney), 55 (volleyball), 75, 78, 80, 85 (Evelyn Glennie), 88 (Gloria), 90 (boy); Imagestate p. 25 (4); John Birdsall Photography p. 35 (schoolgirl); London Features International p. 43 (2, 3); Magnum p. 15 (slum); Mary Evans Picture Library p. 23 (1); Merseyside Photo Library p. 23 (3); The Moviestore Collection p. 88 (Hugh Grant); OUP p. 93 (both); Powerstock pp. 9 (a, c), 34, 70, 83; PYMCA p. 9 (d); Rex Features pp. 9 (b), 20 (removal van), 23 (4), 29, 44 (all), 45 (4, 6), 50 (Henry), 51 (Rupert Grint), 90 (Christina Aguilera).

5

WORKBOOK

INTRODUCTION

VOCABULARY

Revision

Student's Book **page 5**

1 Label the pictures with words from the box. Then put the other words in the correct group.

collecting things fashion funny
generous insensitive magazines
moody music nice pick up
quiet road bikes sensitive take off
turn on

1 personality adjectives ___generous___

______ ______

______ ______

______ ______

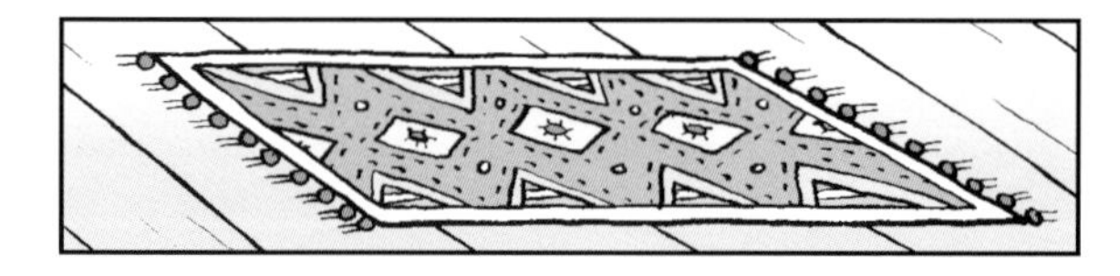

2 phrasal verbs ______

______ ______

3 interests ______

______ ______

______ ______

2 Complete the sentences with words from exercise 1.

1 They love ______ – they go cycling every weekend.
2 Can you ______ the TV? I want to watch the news.
3 Your cousin is very ______ – she never speaks.
4 ______ your shoes when you go into the house. They're dirty.
5 My brother is very ______ – I always laugh at his jokes.
6 She's very ______ – she never thinks before she speaks.
7 I love ______, but I haven't got enough money to buy lots of clothes.

3 Write sentences about you or your friends which include the word in brackets.

(turn on) I turned on the television.

1 (sensitive) ______

______

2 (nice) ______

______

3 (generous) ______

______

4 (music) ______

______

5 (collecting things) ______

______

6 (moody) ______

______

GRAMMAR

Check	Student's Book, pages 6, 8

Present simple

1 Write sentences. Use the present simple affirmative, negative or interrogative.

1 Joanna / watch / police dramas / on TV

____

2 she / live / in a flat or a house?

____

3 we / not have / the same interests

____

4 he / go swimming / on Sundays

____

5 he / have / piano lessons / at school

____

6 they / prefer / rap or heavy metal?

____

7 I / not wear / tracksuits

____

8 she / worry / about everything

____

2 Rewrite the sentences as questions. Then write affirmative or negative short answers.

He likes music.
Does he like music?
Yes, he does.

1 She doesn't wear trendy clothes.

____
____

2 They collect stamps.

____
____

3 He tells a lot of jokes.

____
____

4 They don't go to the library.

____
____

5 Her boyfriend looks nice.

____
____

Present continuous

3 Complete the text. Use the present continuous, affirmative or negative, of the verbs in the box.

chat not get not laugh practise
not rain send stay try watch

Hi Harry

How are you? I (**1**) ____________ you this email because I'm really annoyed. I (**2**) ____________ to do my homework, but I can't concentrate. It's a horrible day – it (**3**) ____________ , but it's very cold and windy – so we're all (**4**) ____________ inside. My brother (**5**) ____________ on the phone to his girlfriend. My mum and dad (**6**) ____________ a comedy on TV, but they (**7**) ____________ very much because it isn't very funny. My sister (**8**) ____________ the piano in the next room. She (**9**) ____________ any better. Help!

Julie

4 Now write questions and answers about Julie and her family.

1 what / Julie / try / to do?

____
____

2 it / rain?

____
____

3 who / her brother / chat / to?

____
____

4 what / her parents / watch?

____
____

5 what / her sister / do?

____
____

Past simple

5 Rewrite the sentences. Change affirmative to negative, or negative to affirmative.

We went to a museum.
We didn't go to a museum.
I didn't have breakfast.
I had breakfast.

1 She didn't know the answer.

____

2 I felt nervous before the exam.

____

3 He didn't get up early this morning.

____

4 You didn't give your sister a birthday present.

____

5 He sat at the front of the class.

____

6 They didn't chat on the phone.

____

Question words

6 Write questions in the past simple. Then write true answers.

1 how many / lessons / you / have / yesterday?

____

____

2 when / you / go to school / this morning?

____

____

3 who / you / phone / yesterday?

____

____

4 which / subjects / you / enjoy / last year?

____

____

5 what / you / eat / last night?

____

____

EVERYDAY ENGLISH

Dialogue

Student's Book page 7

1 Complete the conversation with the words in the box.

for from home if meet new

INTRODUCING PEOPLE

Suzie Jack, this is Victoria. She's (**1**) ____________ .

Jack Hello, Victoria.

Victoria Hi, Jack. Nice to (**2**) ____________ you.

Jack And you.

Suzie Victoria is (**3**) ____________ Scotland.

Victoria We moved here in August.

Jack How come?

Victoria My mum lost her job in Scotland. She's looking (**4**) ____________ a new job here.

Jack Oh, right. Do you miss (**5**) ____________ ?

Victoria Yes, I do. I really miss the mountains and the countryside.

Jack Well, (**6**) ____________ you fancy going for a bike ride, give me a call.

Victoria Thanks! See you around.

2 Answer the questions.

1 Where is Victoria from?

____

2 When did Victoria move?

____

3 Why did Victoria move?

____

4 What two things does Victoria miss about home?

____

5 What does Jack invite Victoria to do?

____

3 Write a conversation in your notebook like the one in exercise 1.

A: Alex, this is Isabel. She's _______________

B: _______________

C: _______________

____

B: _______________

A: _______________

C: _______________

B: _______________

C: _______________

____

____

B: _______________

____

C: _______________

____

B: _______________

____

____

C: _______________

LEARNING DIARY

		Yes	No
Vocabulary	I can name three interests, three phrasal verbs and three personality adjectives.		
Grammar	I can use present simple affirmative, negative and interrogative.		
	I can form and use the present continuous affirmative and negative.		
	I can ask subject and object questions.		
	I can use the past simple affirmative, negative and interrogative.		
	I can make questions with different question words.		
Speaking	I know how to introduce people.		

1 The right image

VOCABULARY

Describing appearance

Student's Book page 9

1 Label the picture with the words in the box.

bracelet dyed hair earring necklace
piercing ring sunglasses tattoo

1 dyed hair
2 ____________
3 ____________
4 ____________
5 ____________
6 ____________
7 ____________
8 ____________

2 Complete the sentences with adjectives that describe appearance.

1 She looks s_ _ _ _y and he looks s_ _ _t .

2 He looks s_ _ _ _ _y and she looks t_ _ _ _y .

3 She looks c_ _ _ _l and he looks o_ _ - _ _ _ _ _ _ _ _d .

Word help *-ed* and *-ing* adjectives

Student's Book page 11

3 Complete the adjectives. Use *-ed* or *-ing*.

1 I was very disappoint______ when I heard Kate wasn't coming to my party.
2 I'm really bor______. Let's do something interest______.
3 The instructions for my new mobile are very confus______.
4 I was surpris______ when I saw he was wearing scruffy clothes.
5 My little sister is really annoy______. She's always taking CDs from my room.
6 I'm not interest______ in fashion.
7 My dog won't bite you. Don't be frighten______.
8 I was really embarrass______ when my mum started singing in the supermarket.

4 Use *-ed* and *-ing* adjectives to describe these things and experiences in your life.

a horror film
It was frightening. But I was also really excited.

1 your English book
____
____

2 a shopping trip
____
____

3 the result of your last exam
____
____

4 a football match
____
____

5 an argument with a friend
____
____

GRAMMAR

Check	Student's Book, pages 12, 14

Present tense contrast

1 Write sentences about what Tom usually does, and what he's doing today.

drink / coffee at breakfast // tea
Tom usually drinks coffee at breakfast, but today he's drinking tea.

1 wear / smart clothes to school // casual clothes
______
______

2 walk / to school // go by bike
______
______

3 have / a sandwich for lunch // a pizza
______
______

4 play / tennis after school // football
______
______

5 watch / TV in the evening // play computer games
______
______

6 go / to bed at eleven o'clock // ten o'clock
______
______

2 Complete the sentences. Use the present simple or present continuous.

1 She ______ (want) to have a tattoo on her arm.

2 'What ______ (we / listen) to?' 'A Jamelia song.'

3 ______ (you / remember) his phone number?

4 It's very cold, but it ______ (not snow).

5 Every week she ______ (buy) a bracelet or a necklace.

6 I ______ (not believe) a word he says!

3 Complete the phone conversation with the verbs in the box. Use the present simple or present continuous.

like look for play want watch not watch wear wear

Chris Hi Sarah. Where are you?
Sarah I'm in town. I (**1**) ______ some earrings.
Chris You never (**2**) ______ earrings.
Sarah Yes, I do. I (**3**) ______ some now! But they're a bit old. I (**4**) ______ some trendier ones. Where are you?
Chris I'm at home. I (**5**) ______ an Arnold Schwarzenegger film. I (**6**) ______ him, but this film's really boring.
Sarah Is Steven there?
Chris Yes, but he (**7**) ______ the film. He (**8**) ______ computer games upstairs.
Sarah I'm in the shop now. I'll call you back later!
Chris Bye.

4 Complete the sentences. Use the present simple in one sentence and the present continuous in the other.

1 enjoy
a) I ______ this pizza. It's delicious.
b) I ______ watching TV on Friday evenings.

2 work
a) My dad ______ in a bank.
b) Be quiet. I ______ .

3 rain
a) Oh, no! It ______ . And we're having a barbecue this afternoon!
b) It ______ a lot in India.

4 try
a) Be quiet! I ______ to watch this film.
b) I always ______ to get up before seven o'clock.

EVERYDAY ENGLISH

like/hate, etc. + gerund

5 Complete the sentences. Use the gerund of the verb in brackets and your own ideas.

1 I hate (do)

____

____

2 My parents enjoy (watch) ______________

____

3 My best friend doesn't like (wear) ________

____

4 I love (eat) ______________________

____

5 I don't mind (go)

____

but I prefer (go)

____

Subject and object questions

6 Write questions with *what* or *who*.

Somebody phoned Tom.
Who phoned Tom?
Jo ate **something**.
What did Jo eat?

1 **Something** fell on my foot.

____

2 They sent **something** to their grandparents.

____

3 Margaret bought **something** in town.

____

4 **Somebody** stole Jenny's bracelet.

____

5 Sam met **somebody** in the park.

____

6 **Somebody** invited you to the party.

____

7 **Somebody** sent Rachel an email.

____

Dialogue

Student's Book page 13

1 Read the conversation. Which is true?

Mark, Sue and Vicky are going to listen to music at (**a**) Vicky's house (**b**) Liz's house.

MAKING ARRANGEMENTS

Dad 493633. Hello.
Sue Oh, hello. Can I speak to Mark, please?
Dad Yes. Who's calling, please?
Sue It's Sue.
Dad Just a moment. I'll get him.
Mark Hello, Sue. How are you?
Sue I'm OK, thanks. And you?
Mark Fine.
Sue Listen, Mark. Are you doing anything tomorrow evening?
Mark No, nothing special. Why?
Sue I'm going round to Vicky's house. We're going to listen to some CDs. Would you like to come?
Mark I'd love to. Is Liz going too?
Sue No, I don't think so.
Mark What time are you going?
Sue At about seven.
Mark OK. I'll call for you on the way.

2 Correct the sentences.

1 Mark rings Sue.

____

2 Mark's mum answers the phone.

____

3 Mark is busy tomorrow evening.

____

4 They're going to watch some DVDs.

____

5 Sue will call for Mark on the way.

____

3 Write a conversation in your notebook like the one in exercise 1.

READING AND WRITING

Reading

4 **Read the text. Match the headings (1–3) with the paragraphs (A–C).**

1 Personality	
2 Image	
3 One thing he loves and one thing he hates	

This is my best friend
by Cathy

[**A**] My best friend is called Sam. I think he's very trendy and he likes fashion. Sometimes he wears quite unusual or scruffy clothes, but he always looks cool. He's got dark hair, but he has dyed some of it blonde. He's got an earring in one ear. However, he doesn't wear any other jewellery.

[**B**] He's quite an independent person. He's quiet and he enjoys being alone. On the other hand, he's also friendly and he's got a good sense of humour. The only bad thing is that he's sometimes a bit moody and can get annoyed easily.

[**C**] One thing he loves is playing the guitar. He's really good and he practises a lot, although he doesn't play in a band. One thing he hates is going out with very large groups of people. He prefers going out with two or three friends.

5 **Find five more adjectives that Cathy uses to describe Sam.**

trendy
1 ______________
2 ______________
3 ______________
4 ______________
5 ______________

6 **Correct these sentences.**

1 Cathy thinks Sam is old-fashioned.
____
2 Sam always wears smart clothes.
____
3 Sam never wears jewellery.
____
4 Sam never gets annoyed.
____
5 Sam plays the piano.
____
6 Sam likes going out with large groups.
____

Writing Expressing contrast

Student's Book page 16

7 **Underline these words in the text in exercise 4: *but*, *although*, *however*, *on the other hand*.**

8 **Complete the sentences. Use the words in the boxes. Add commas where necessary.**

although on the other hand

1 He wears smart clothes to school, ______________ he prefers wearing scruffy clothes.
2 I'd like to go to the cinema this evening. ______________ I don't want to miss the Liverpool match on TV.
3 Pete loves rap music, ______________ he doesn't like Eminem.

but however

4 She wears make-up, ______________ she never wears jewellery.
5 She's very friendly. ______________ she's sometimes a bit moody, too.
6 He loves playing the guitar. ______________ he isn't very good.

9 Write notes for these three paragraphs about your best friend or someone you know very well.

Paragraph 1
Name: ____________________
Image: trendy / old-fashioned / cool? etc. ____________________
Hair / eyes / jewellery / make-up / tattoos / piercings? ____________________
Clothes: what does he/she wear? sporty / casual / scruffy? etc. ____________________

Paragraph 2
What kind of person is he/she? ____________________
friendly? quiet? cheerful? moody? etc. ____________________
Bad things? ____________________

Paragraph 3
Something he/she loves ____________________
Something he/she hates ____________________
He/she prefers …? ____________________

10 Write a text in your notebook. Use your notes from exercise 9 and the writing guide.

Paragraph 1
My best friend …
I think he/she's …
He/She's got …
He/She wears …

Paragraph 2
He/She's a … person.
However, he/she's …
The only bad thing is …

Paragraph 3
One thing he/she loves is …
One thing he/she hates …

LEARNING DIARY

		Yes	No
Vocabulary	I can name five accessories you put on and take off.		
	I can describe someone's general appearance.		
Grammar	I know when to use present simple and when to use present continuous.		
	I can make sentences with *like/hate* + gerund.		
	I can ask subject and object questions.		
Pronunciation	I know where to put the stress on two and three syllable words.		
Speaking	I know how to make arrangements.		
Writing	I can write nine sentences about myself.		

VOCABULARY

The urban landscape

Student's Book page 17

1 Complete the descriptions with the words in the box.

advertisements block of flats bridge car park factory motorway pavement post box railway recycling bins street lamps traffic lights

1 There's a ________ that is nearly empty. There are some ________ in one corner, and there's a ________ with two trains. Behind, there's a ________ .

2 There's a wide ________ . A ________ goes over it. There are lots of ________ and two big ________ .

3 There's a tall ________ . Some people are walking along the ________ . A girl is posting a letter in the ________ . A car is waiting at the ________ .

2 Complete the definitions with words from exercise 1.

1 Trains go along a ________ .
2 You can leave your car in a ________ .
3 A ________ is a tall building where people live.
4 You put letters in a ________ .
5 You use a ________ to cross a road, a river or a valley.
6 A ________ is a large road between cities.
7 A ________ is a big building where things are manufactured.

3 Now write definitions for two more words from exercise 1.

1 ____

____

2 ____

____

Word help Extreme adjectives

Student's Book page 19

4 Rewrite the sentences. Use extreme adjectives.

His sister is very beautiful.
His sister is gorgeous.

1 This song is good.
____
2 It's very cold today.
____
3 Your trainers are very dirty.
____
4 When's lunch? I'm hungry.
____
5 That dog is very big.
____
6 His hair looks bad.
____

GRAMMAR

Check	Student's Book, pages 20, 22 Irregular verbs, page 56

Past simple and past continuous

1 **What were they doing when the accident happened? Write sentences.**

Robert / chat / on the phone
Robert was chatting on the phone.

1 Jim and Isabel / cross / the road

____

2 Sarah / wait / at the traffic lights

____

3 Gloria / come / out of the car park

____

4 Ali and Raquel / sit / on the bus

____

5 Paula / read / an advertisement

____

2 **Complete the questions. Then write affirmative or negative answers.**

Were the cars *going* (go) very fast?

Yes, *they were.*

1 ______ a lot of people __________ (stand) on the pavement?

Yes, ______________________________

2 ______ it __________ (get) dark?

No, ______________________________

3 ______ the drivers __________ (watch) the road?

No, ______________________________

3 **Complete the sentences. Use the past simple and past continuous.**

1 We __________ (walk) along the pavement when we __________ (see) the advertisement.

2 He __________ (break) his arm while he __________ (play) rugby.

3 They __________ (not enjoy) the party when I __________ (arrive).

4 My parents __________ (meet) each other when they __________ (work) in the same factory.

5 She __________ (not wear) a coat when she __________ (leave) home.

4 **Complete the texts with the past simple and past continuous.**

Memories

My first day at school

It (**1**) __________ (rain) when my mum and I (**2**) __________ (arrive) at the school gates. We (**3**) __________ (run) into the school. In the classroom there were lots of children. They (**4**) __________ (not sit) at their desks. They (**5**) __________ (stand) around the teacher. I (**6**) __________ (be) terrified. While I (**7**) __________ (watch) the other children, my mum (**8**) __________ (kiss) me and (**9**) __________ (say) goodbye.

The moment I first saw my boyfriend

One morning, I (**10**) __________ (go) into the classroom early. I (**11**) __________ (get) my book out of my bag when a new student (**12**) __________ (come) in. He (**13**) __________ (wear) jeans and a trendy jacket. He (**14**) __________ (not say) anything, but he (**15**) __________ (smile) at me. I (**16**) __________ (know) immediately that I liked him.

used to

5 Complete the first part of the sentences (1–6) using *used to*. Then match them with the second part (a–f).

1 He ____________ (be) a farmer,

2 We ____________ (live) in the same block of flats as our cousins,

3 I ____________ (like) Robbie Williams,

4 My street ____________ (be) very dark at night,

5 They ____________ (skateboard) on the pavement,

6 She ____________ (work) in a hospital,

a) but his last CD wasn't very good.

b) but we moved.

c) but now they go to the park.

d) but now he works in a factory.

e) but now she's a bus driver.

f) but now there are street lamps.

6 Complete sentences. Use the negative form of *used to*.

I like jazz now, but I didn't use to like it.

1 She reads magazines now, but

______________________________ them.

2 We visit my grandmother now, but

______________________________ her.

3 You wear hats now, but

______________________________ them.

4 He does his homework now, but

______________________________ it.

5 I send text messages now, but

______________________________ them.

6 She likes him now, but

______________________________ him.

EVERYDAY ENGLISH

Dialogue

Student's Book page 21

1 Complete the conversation. Use the words in the box.

great heavy like old what you

EXPRESSING LIKES AND DISLIKES

Peter What shall we listen to?

Megan Have a look through the CDs.

Peter Oh, you've got a D12 CD. They're a (**1**) ________ band. I love Eminem.

Megan Do (**2**) ________ ? I used to like him, but I've gone off him a bit.

Peter What about the Black Eyed Peas?

Megan No, I listened to them all day yesterday! How about Limp Bizkit. Do you (**3**) ________ Fred Durst?

Peter He's not bad. Oh, this is good: Metallica.

Megan That's my brother's. I'm not very keen on (**4**) ________ metal.

Peter Well, (**5**) ________ shall we listen to?

Megan There's *Twentysomething*, the Jamie Cullum album.

Peter That's so (**6**) ________ ! And I can't stand jazz.

Megan OK. Let's listen to D12 then.

2 Answer the questions.

1 What does Peter think of Eminem?

____

2 Why doesn't Megan want to listen to the Black Eyed Peas or Metallica?

____

3 What is Peter's opinion of jazz?

____

3 Write a conversation in your notebook like the one in exercise 1.

READING AND WRITING

Reading

4 **Read the text. Which of these hasn't changed very much?**

a) Veronica's school life.
b) Veronica's clothes.
c) Veronica's hair.

Changes by Veronica

1 ____________

I've changed a lot in the past five years. I look different, I do different things and I have different opinions.

2 ____________

My hair used to be short, but now it's quite long. I didn't used to wear jewellery, but now I often wear earrings, bracelets and rings. My style of clothes hasn't changed very much. I still wear casual clothes: jeans, T-shirts, tracksuits, things like that.

3 ____________

Five years ago, I didn't go to this school. I was at primary school. My favourite subject was English. Now, I prefer sciences. We didn't use to get any homework at primary school but now we get lots!

4 ____________

I didn't use to go out in the evenings. I used to stay at home and watch TV with my parents. Now I often meet my friends in town. At weekends, I usually go shopping. Five years ago, I used to go swimming with my brothers.

5 ____________

I think my life is better now than it was five years ago. Although I have to work harder, I'm more independent and I've got more friends.

5 **Are these sentences true or false about Veronica now?**

1 She's got short hair. ________
2 She often wears earrings. ________
3 She wears casual clothes. ________
4 She doesn't get homework. ________
5 She usually goes shopping at weekends. ________
6 She's more independent. ________

Writing Structuring an essay

Student's Book page 24

6 **Match the paragraphs (1–5) in exercise 4 with five of the headings in the box.**

School Introduction Likes and dislikes
Conclusion Appearance Free time
Home and family

7 **Write notes for a text about how your life has changed. Start with the Introduction and end with the Conclusion. Choose three other headings from exercise 6.**

Paragraph 1: Introduction

____
____
____
____
____

Paragraph 2: ____________

____
____
____
____
____

Paragraph 3: ________
____
____
____
____
____

Paragraph 4: ________
____
____
____
____
____

Paragraph 5: Conclusion
____
____
____
____
____

8 Write a text in your notebook. Use your notes from exercise 7 and the writing guide.

Paragraph 1
I've changed / I haven't changed ...

Paragraph 2
I used to / didn't use to ... . Now ...

Paragraph 3
Five years ago, I ... but now ...

Paragraph 4
I used to / didn't use to ... . Now ...

Paragraph 5
I think my life is ... now than five years ago. (Why?)

LEARNING DIARY

		Yes	No
Vocabulary	I can name seven things in a town.		
Grammar	I know when to use past simple and when to use past continuous.		
	I can talk about the past using *used to.*		
Pronunciation	I can make exclamations with the correct stress and intonation.		
Speaking	I know how to express likes and dislikes.		
Writing	I can write twelve sentences about where I live.		

VOCABULARY

The senses

Student's Book page 25

1 **Label the five senses (1–5). Then complete the verbs in each sentence.**

1 hearing

Stop singing! That song sounds terrible!

2 ____________

This pizza t____________ great! Can I have another one?

3 ____________

I don't understand this painting. It l____________ strange.

4 ____________

You can't wear these socks again. They s____________ horrible!

5 ____________

Be careful! The cup f____________ very hot.

2 **Write sentences with the words in the box. Use *like / don't like* and *smell*, *taste* or *sound*.**

birds singing eggs fresh bread hot dogs rain strong cheese

I like the smell of fresh bread.

1 ____

____

2 ____

____

3 ____

____

4 ____

____

Word help Words that are verbs and nouns

Student's Book page 27

3 **Complete the sentences with the words in the box. Then decide if they are verbs or nouns.**

dance dream drink ~~help~~ sleep snow swim

Can you help me with my homework, please? (verb)

1 I had a horrible ____________ last night. A man was chasing me, but I woke up before he caught me. ____________

2 My sister studies music and ____________ at the School of Performing Arts in Liverpool. ____________

3 I can't ____________ this coffee. It tastes awful! ____________

4 In the winter does it ____________ a lot in Scotland? ____________

5 We went to the beach, but we didn't go for a ____________ . ____________

6 If I can't ____________ , I get up and make myself a cup of tea. ____________

GRAMMAR

Check	Student's Book pages 28, 30 Irregular Verbs page 56

Present perfect affirmative and negative

1 Write the past simple forms and past participles of these irregular verbs.

Past simple	Past participle
was/were	**1**
2	broken
got	**3**
4	known
put	**5**
6	slept

2 Complete the sentences. Use the present perfect affirmative.

1 Oh no! I ____________ (drop) my sandwich.

2 We ____________ (have) three lessons this morninng.

3 She ____________ (go) to Paris three times.

4 I ____________ (tidy) my bedroom.

5 England ____________ (win) the World Cup once.

6 Oh no! We ____________ (miss) the bus.

3 Complete the sentences with the verbs in the box. Use the present perfect negative.

do go hear listen take write

1 I ________________ Anastacia's new CD. Is it good?

2 She ________________ an email.

3 They ________________ the shopping.

4 We ________________ snorkelling.

5 He ________________ the rubbish out.

6 You ________________ to a word I've said!

4 Complete the text. Use the present perfect affirmative or negative.

Marie Duval is a professional snowboarder. This year she (**1**) ________ (do) a lot of training, mostly in France. But she (**2**) ________ also ____________ (visit) Switzerland. She (**3**) ____________ (participate) in five or six competitions, but she (**4**) ____________ (not win) any. 'This year I (**5**) ____________ (go) snowboarding a lot,' she says,' but luckily I (**6**) ____________ (not have) any injuries.'

5 Look at John's list. Write sentences with the present perfect affirmative and negative.

Things to do
1 make my bed ✗
2 tidy my room ✗
3 do my homework ✓
4 go shopping ✗
5 meet Harry ✓
6 buy Jamelia's latest CD ✗
7 write an email to Kate ✓

1 John hasn't made his bed.

2 ________________________________

3 ________________________________

4 ________________________________

5 ________________________________

6 ________________________________

____

7 ________________________________

6 **What is *She's* in each sentence? Write *She is* or *She has*.**

She's finished her homework. She has

She's going to the cinema. She is

1 She's got a new computer. ________
2 She's been to Italy. ________
3 She's done the washing up. ________
4 She's hungry. ________
5 She's going skiing. ________
6 She's left the house. ________
7 She's tidied her room. ________
8 She's tidying her room. ________

Present perfect with *just*

7 **Write sentences with the present perfect and *just*. Use the verbs in brackets.**

'Is John here yet?'

'Yes, he's just arrived.' (arrive)

1 'Are you hungry?'
'No, ________________________' (eat)
2 'Don't forget to do your homework.'
'________________________ it.' (do)
3 'Is Sarah still here?'
'No, ________________________' (leave)
4 'What happened to your glasses?'
'________________________ them.' (break)
5 'Don't forget to phone your grandad.'
'________________________ him.' (phone)
6 'Are Chelsea winning the match?'
'Yes, ________________________' (score)
7 'Did your cousin send you a letter?'
'Yes, ________________________ it.' (get)
8 'Are you thirsty?'
'No, ________________________ a drink.' (have)

EVERYDAY ENGLISH

Dialogue

Student's Book page 29

1 **Complete the conversation. Use the words in the box.**

antibiotics have infection taken times well

AT THE DOCTOR'S

Doctor Hello, Helen. How are you?
Helen I don't feel very (**1**) ________ . I've got a sore throat.
Doctor How long (**2**) ________ you had it?
Helen Um, it started two days ago, on Monday.
Doctor I see. Have you (**3**) ________ any medication for it?
Helen No, not really. Just a painkiller this morning.
Doctor Let me have a look. You've got an (**4**) ________ . I'll prescribe some (**5**) ________ . They should help.
Helen Thanks.
Doctor Take them three (**6**) ________ a day, before meals.
Helen OK. Thank you, doctor. Goodbye.
Doctor Goodbye.

2 **Answer the questions.**

1 What's Helen's problem?
____
2 How long has she had it?
____
3 Has she taken any painkillers?
____
4 What does the doctor prescribe?
____

3 **Write a conversation in your notebook like the one in exercise 1.**

READING AND WRITING

Reading

4 **Read the text. Match the paragraphs (A–D) with the headings in the box.**

Achievements   Early years
Hobbies and interests   Introduction

Evelyn Glennie

A ____________________

Evelyn Glennie is one of the most famous musicians in the world. The amazing thing about her is that she is almost totally deaf.

B ____________________

Evelyn Glennie was born in Aberdeen, Scotland, in 1965. As a young child, she loved music and learnt to play the piano. When she was eight she began to lose her hearing, and by the age of twelve she was profoundly deaf. But instead of giving up her love of music, she started to learn the drums and other percussion instruments. She can't hear the music, but she feels the rhythm.

C ____________________

Evelyn has recorded eighteen CDs, and gives about 110 concerts a year all over the world. She has won a lot of awards for her playing, including a Grammy. In 1991, Evelyn published her best-selling autobiography *Good Vibrations*.

D ____________________

In her spare time, Evelyn loves to draw and paint. She also makes and collects musical instruments. She's got over 1,800 of them! She also loves playing computer games.

5 **Answer the questions.**

1 Why is Evelyn Glennie amazing?

____

2 When and where was she born?

____

3 How old was she when she became profoundly deaf?

____

4 How many CDs has she recorded?

____

5 What famous music award has she won?

____

6 What is the name of her autobiography?

____

7 Name three of her hobbies.

____

Writing Brainstorming

Student's Book **page 32**

6 **Complete the notes about Erik Weihenmeyer using the information in the boxes.**

Paragraph A: Introduction

famous mountaineer   totally blind

(1) Job ____________________
(2) Why is that amazing? ____________________
____

Paragraph B: Early years

climbing   USA   sight   sport   13
1968

(3) Born (When? Where?) ________ / ________

(4) As a child, what did he love? ________

(5) What did he lose? ________

(6) Totally blind – at what age? ________

(7) What did he start when he was 16? ________

Paragraph C: Achievements

climbed highest mountain on each continent
climb Mount Everest 'Free Spirit Award'
Top of the World

(8) First blind person to ________

(9) Other achievement? ________

(10) Awards? ________

(11) Autobiography ________

Paragraph D: Hobbies and interests

running marathons skiing sky-diving

(12) Hobbies and interests ________

____

7 **Write a biography of Erik Weihenmeyer in your notebook. Use the notes, the text in exercise 4 and the writing guide.**

Paragraph A: Introduction
Erik Weihenmeyer is one of ...
The amazing thing ...

Paragraph B
Erik was born ... As a young child, ...
By the age of ...
But instead of ...

Paragraph C
Erik was the first blind ...
He has also ... He has won ...
In ... he published ...

Paragraph D
In his spare time ...

LEARNING DIARY

		Yes	No
Vocabulary	I can name the five senses and use them to describe things.		
Grammar	I can make positive and negative sentences in present perfect.		
	I can use present perfect with *just*.		
Pronunciation	I can pronounce groups of consonants correctly.		
Speaking	I know what to say at the doctor's.		
Writing	I can write seven sentences about my memories of smells and sounds.		

VOCABULARY

Relationships and dating

Student's Book **page 37**

1 Complete the conversation. Use the words and phrases in the box.

ask (somebody) out   fall in love
fancy   go out   have an argument
meet   split up

Sue How did you and Tim (**1**) __________?
Emily We were both at my cousin's Christmas party last year.
Sue Did you (**2**) __________ him when you first saw him?
Emily Yes, I thought he was attractive.
Sue When did he (**3**) __________ you __________?
Emily He didn't – I did it! I phoned him the day after the party.
Sue Well done! Did you (**4**) __________ on the first date?
Emily Not really, but we had a good time. We went for a burger. After that, we started to (**5**) __________ every weekend – to the cinema, parties, discos ...
Sue Why did you (**6**) __________?
Emily I'm not sure. We didn't (**7**) __________ or a fight – but now we're together again.

2 Label the pictures in the correct order.

1b, ...

3 Complete the story of Emily and Tim. Use the past simple of the verbs in the box.

go out   get engaged   get married
make up

Emily and Tim (**1**) __________ in the spring and started to (**2**) __________ __________ again. They went on holiday to Paris and they (**3**) __________ in front of the Eiffel tower. A few months later, they (**4**) __________ at a beautiful castle by a lake.

Word help Noun endings: *-ion* and *-ment*

Student's Book **page 39**

4 Make the verbs in the box into nouns. Use the nouns to complete the text.

advertise   arrange   celebrate
disappoint   discuss   embarrass
entertain

When Jane and Martin got married, there was a big (**1**) __________ with a hundred guests. Jane's uncle couldn't go because he had another (**2**) __________ for that day. That was a big (**3**) __________ for Jane because she loves her uncle.

Jane and Martin wanted to have a band at the wedding to provide the (**4**) __________ but they couldn't agree on the style of music. After a long (**5**) __________, they decided to choose a rock and roll band. They looked in the newspaper and found an (**6**) __________ for a band called Pink Cadillac. The band was terrible and all the guests laughed. It was an (**7**) __________ for Jane and Martin!

GRAMMAR

Check	Student's Book pages 40, 42 Irregular verbs page 56

Present perfect interrogative

1 Write the past participles.

be *been*

1	chat	______	7	learn	______
2	choose	______	8	make	______
3	eat	______	9	meet	______
4	finish	______	10	read	______
5	have	______	11	see	______
6	know	______	12	stop	______

2 Complete the questions and short answers. Use the present perfect.

Have you seen (you / see) the new Hugh Grant film?

Yes, *I have*.

1 ______ (he / read) the script?

No, ______ .

2 ______ (they / eat) their dinner?

Yes, ______ .

3 ______ (you / meet) my cousin?

No, ______ .

4 ______ (she / finish) her homework?

Yes, ______ .

5 ______ (it / stop) raining?

Yes, ______ .

3 Look at the list. Then write questions and short answers about Gloria Goldberg.

<u>Gloria's list of things to do</u>
1 read the script ✓
2 learn her lines ✗
3 visit the studio ✓
4 see the set ✓
5 choose her costume ✗
6 meet the director ✓
7 chat to the other actors ✗

1 *Has she read the script?*
Yes, she has.

2 ______________________
____

3 ______________________
____

4 ______________________
____

5 ______________________
____

6 ______________________
____

7 ______________________
____

for and *since*

4 Complete the sentences with *for* or *since*.

1 I haven't been to the cinema ______ six months.

2 She's had that bike ______ she was twelve years old.

3 You haven't phoned me ______ ages.

4 He's been famous ______ he was a child.

5 They've lived abroad ______ Christmas.

6 She's been my favourite actress ______ years.

EVERYDAY ENGLISH

How long ...?

5 **Write questions with *How long ...*? Then write true answers with *for* or *since*.**

1 ______________________________
______________ (you / have) this book?
____

2 ______________________________
________ (your best friend / be) a student?
____

3 ______________________________
_________ (you / live) in your house or flat?
____

4 ______________________________
_____________ (your teacher / know) you?
____

6 **Complete the interview with Gloria Goldberg. Use the present perfect interrogative and *for* or *since*.**

Interviewer (**1**) ______________________
(you / make) a film in England before?

Gloria No, I haven't. This is my first visit.

Interviewer (**2**) ______________________
________ (how long / you / be) here?

Gloria (**3**) ________ a week. I love it! I've met some really nice people (**4**) ____________ I arrived. And it's great to work with Julia Roberts again.

Interviewer (**5**) ______________________
(how long / she / be) a friend?

Gloria (**6**) ________ 2002. We made a film together in Hollywood.

Interview (**7**) ______________________
(Julia / arrive) in England too?

Gloria Yes, she has. She's been here (**8**) ________ Wednesday.

Interview (**9**) ______________________
(you and Julia / met) the other actors?

Gloria No, we haven't. Julia has only been here (**10**) ________ three days!

Dialogue

Student's Book **page 41**

1 **Put the words in the correct order to make questions. Then write them in the correct place in the conversation.**

drink / to / anything ?
pasta / of / day / the / the / what's ?
you / to drink / would / what / like ?
order / can / take / your / I ?
you / decided / and / yet / have ?

AT A RESTAURANT

Waiter (**1**) ______________________ ?
Joanna I haven't made up my mind yet.
Dermot Oh, OK, I'll go first.
(**2**) ______________________ ?
Waiter It's spaghetti with mushrooms.
Dermot OK, I'll have the tomato soup to start, followed by the steak, please.
Waiter Fine. (**3**) ______________________ ?
Dermot Yes, please. Water.
Waiter Sparkling or still?
Dermot Sparkling, please.
Waiter Good. (**4**) ______________________ ?
Joanna I'll have the vegetable pâté to start, followed by the salmon.
Waiter (**5**) ______________________ ?
Joanna Lemonade, please.
Waiter Thank you!

2 **What do Joanna and Dermot order? Write *J* or *D* next to the food and drink.**

Starters
tomato soup ______ melon ______
chicken soup ______ vegetable pâté ______

Main courses
roast lamb ______ grilled salmon ______
steak and chips ______ pasta of the day ______

Drinks
sparkling water ______ lemonade ______
still water ______ milk ______

3 **Write a conversation in your notebook like the one in exercise 1.**

READING AND WRITING

Reading

4 **Read the text. Where do Malcolm and Christina go on their date? Put the places in the correct order from 1–3.**

an art gallery a barbecue a cinema
a disco a football match a party
a pop concert a restaurant

My imaginary date
by Malcolm

Two weeks ago, I met Christina Aguilera in a shopping centre in London. We chatted for a while. Then I asked her out and she said yes! I was really excited because I've been a fan for years.

We went out together last Saturday night. I picked her up in a taxi at seven o'clock and we went for a meal in a restaurant. I had steak and chips. Christina had a chicken salad.

After dinner, we went to the cinema and saw the new Jackie Chan film. I love Jackie Chan. Both Christina and I really enjoyed it.

At eleven o'clock, we went to a disco. I'm not a great dancer, but Christina didn't mind. We stayed until it closed. Neither Christina nor I wanted to leave! At the end of the date, we said goodnight and I got a taxi home.

It was a fantastic date. Christina has given me her phone number in the USA. I'll call her when I go there on holiday.

5 **Answer the questions.**

1 When did Malcolm meet Christina?

____

2 Why was Malcolm excited about the date?

____

3 What time did Malcolm pick her up?

____

4 How did Malcolm get home after the date?

____

5 When will Malcolm call Christina?

____

Writing *both ... and ..., neither ... nor*

Student's Book page 44

6 **Underline an example of *both ... and ...*, and an example of *neither ... nor ...* in the text in exercise 4.**

7 **Join the sentences. Use *both ... and ...* or *neither ... nor ...* .**

Jack likes skiing. Penny likes skiing.
Both Jack and Penny like skiing.
Jack doesn't dance. Penny doesn't dance.
Neither Jack nor Penny dances.

1 Hannah does karate. I do karate.

____

2 Greta lives in London. Her brother lives in London.

____

3 Karen doesn't eat meat. Ben doesn't eat meat.

____

4 My dad has got blue eyes. My mum has got blue eyes.

____

5 Frank didn't see the film. I didn't see the film.

____

8 Write notes about an imaginary date. Use ideas from exercise 4 or invent your own.

Paragraph 1

Who with? ____________________

Where did you meet him / her? ____________________

How did you feel? Why? ____________________

Paragraph 2

Where did you go first? ____________________

What did you do there? ____________________

Paragraph 3

Where did you go next? ____________________

What did you do there? ____________________

After that, where did you go? ____________________

What did you do there? ____________________

How did the date end? ____________________

Paragraph 4

What has happened since the date?

____

9 Write a text about your imaginary date in your notebook. Use your notes from exercise 8 and the writing guide.

Paragraph 1

... ago, I met ... in ... .

(What happened? How did you feel?)

Paragraph 2

We went out together ...

(Where did you go? What did you do?)

Paragraph 3

After ... , we went to ...

(Where did you go? What did you do?)

At ... o'clock, we went to ...

(Where did you go? What did you do?)

At the end of the date, we ...

Paragraph 4

It was a fantastic / terrible date ...

(What has happened since the date?)

LEARNING DIARY

		Yes	No
Vocabulary	I know seven verb phrases that describe stages in relationships.		
Grammar	I know how to make questions in present perfect.		
	I can use present perfect with *for* and *since*.		
	I can ask questions in present perfect with *How long ...?*		
Pronunciation	I can pronounce *–ought* and *–aught* endings correctly.		
Speaking	I know how to order something at a restaurant.		
Writing	I can describe the history of a couple's relationship.		

VOCABULARY

Jobs

Student's Book **page 45**

1 Read the sentences and complete the puzzle. Don't forget the key word!

1 I put out fires in emergencies. What am I?
2 I take tourists round famous cities. What am I?
3 When animals are sick, I try to make them better. What am I?
4 I often work in bathrooms and kitchens. What am I?
5 When people have legal problems I try to help them. What am I?
6 I wear a uniform. Sometimes I have to fight for my country. What am I?
7 I work in a shop. People give me money when they buy things. What am I?
8 I design buildings like houses, offices and blocks of flats. What am I?

Mystery word I work for a big football club. I help the players to train. What am I?

?
1 F _ _ _ F _ _ _ _ _ _
2 T _ _ _ _ _ _ _ _
3 V _ _
4 P _ _ _ _ _ _
5 L _ _ _ _ _
6 S _ _ _ _ _ _
7 C _ _ _ _ _ _
8 A _ _ _ _ _ _ _ _

2 Write sentences like the ones in exercise 1 for these jobs.

1 surgeon
____
____

2 chef
____
____

3 flight attendant
____
____

Word help Suffixes: *-er*, *-or* and *-ist* for people

Student's Book **page 47**

3 Add *-er*, *-or* or *-ist* to the words in the box. Then use them to complete the sentences.

direct____	inspect____	journal____
pian____	plumb____	reception____
soldi____	translat____	wait____

1 Ask the ____________ for another Cola.
2 Madonna is a good singer and a good ____________.
3 We watched a film about a police ____________ who disappears.
4 We needed a ____________ to repair our shower.
5 My cousin speaks four languages and works as a ____________.
6 My uncle is a ____________ in the army.
7 Stephen Spielberg is my favourite ____________.
8 My dad's a ____________ on our local newspaper.
9 My aunt is a ____________ in a big hotel.

GRAMMAR

Check	Student's Book, pages 48, 50

Comparative and superlative adjectives

1 **Compare the jobs. Use the comparative form of the adjectives in brackets. Give your opinions.**

firefighter / soldier (dangerous)
I think the firefighter has got a more dangerous job than the soldier.

1 flight attendant / tour guide (easy)
___
___

2 coach / architect (interesting)
___
___

3 surgeon / vet (difficult)
___
___

4 receptionist / cashier (boring)
___
___

5 chemist / police inspector (safe)
___
___

6 soldier / plumber (dirty)
___
___

2 **Now write sentences using the superlative form of the adjectives. Give your opinions.**

(easy / subject) *I think geography is the easiest subject in the world!*

1 (beautiful / actress) ___
___

2 (funny / TV programme) ___
___

3 (honest / politician) ___
___

4 (bad / singer) ___
___

5 (handsome / actor) ___
___

6 (good / pop group) ___
___

not as ... as

3 **Complete the sentences. Use *as* or *than*.**

1 I'm taller ___ you.

2 Ben isn't as thin ___ Len.

3 He was happier yesterday ___ he is today.

4 Oxford isn't as exciting ___ London.

5 My job isn't as interesting ___ yours.

6 Kate is more intelligent ___ Sue.

4 **Write sentences. Use *not as ... as*.**

heavy light ~~old~~ poor
rich short tall young

	Sally	Vicky
Age	18	21
Height	165 cm	150 cm
Weight	56 kg	64 kg
Salary	£450	£700

Sally isn't as old as Vicky.

1 ___

2 ___

3 ___

4 ___

5 ___

6 ___

7 ___

EVERYDAY ENGLISH

Expressing result: *so* and *such*

5 Complete the sentences. Use *so* or *such*.

1. This is ________ a good film. You must watch it.
2. I'm ________ hungry! Let's have lunch.
3. It was ________ a hot day that we went to the beach.
4. She was ________ angry that she wouldn't talk to him.
5. His results were ________ bad that he had to take the exam again.
6. This is ________ an easy exercise!

6 Join the two sentences with *so … that*.

I felt very tired. I fell asleep.
I felt so tired that I fell asleep.

1. We were very late. We missed the bus.
____
____
2. The shoes were very expensive. I couldn't afford them.
____
____
3. The coach was very angry. He shouted at his players.
____
____

7 Join the two sentences with *such … that*.

It was a very good book. I couldn't stop reading it.
It was such a good book that I couldn't stop reading it.

1. It was a brilliant party. I didn't want to go home.
____
____
2. It was a very boring film. We left before the end.
____
____
3. It was very cold weather. The car wouldn't start.
____
____

Dialogue

Student's Book page 49

1 Complete the conversation with the words in the box.

40p parcel scales send
slower stamp

AT THE POST OFFICE

Clerk Next, please.
Girl Hello. I'd like to send this (**1**) __________ to Ireland, please.
Clerk Can you put it on the (**2**) __________ , please? … Airmail is £8.30. Surface mail is cheaper: £4.42.
Girl Is surface mail much (**3**) __________?
Clerk It'll take about two weeks.
Girl OK, I'll (**4**) __________ it by surface mail.
Clerk Anything else I can do for you?
Girl Yes, I'd like a (**5**) __________ for this letter, please.
Clerk Where are you sending it?
Girl To Spain.
Clerk OK, that's (**6**) __________ , please.

2 Answer the questions.

1. Where does the girl want to send the parcel to?
____
2. How much is it by airmail?
____
3. How much is it by surface mail?
____
4. What else does the girl want to send?
____

3 Write a conversation in your notebook like the one in exercise 1.

READING AND WRITING

Reading

4 Read the advertisement. What job is being advertised?

> **Computer World**
>
> We are looking for two shop assistants to help in our busy shop. Applicants must be over 15, polite, and preferably know a lot about computer games.
>
> **Write to: Computer World, Milton Retail Park, Bristol BS1 5TF**

> 12 Newtown Rd
> Bristol BS8 5RG
> 25th March 2006
>
> Computer World
> Milton Retail Park
> Bristol BS1 5TF
>
> Dear Sir or Madam,
>
> I saw your advertisement in the local newspaper. I am writing to apply for a job as a shop assistant in your shop.
>
> I am 16 years old and go to St Martin's School. I am a member of the Computer Club at school. When I leave school, I am planning to study computer science at university. My teachers say I am very responsible and friendly.
>
> I am very interested in computer games and often play them on my own and with my friends. My favourite game is Fifa 2005. I will be able to help people to find the best game for them.
>
> At the moment, I'm working in a fast-food restaurant. But working in a computer shop will be much more exciting and interesting.
>
> The earliest date that I could start is 15th April.
>
> I look forward to hearing from you.
>
> Yours faithfully,
>
> *Mark Stephens*
>
> Mark Stephens

5 **Read the advertisement and the letter. Answer the questions.**

1 How many shop assistants are Computer World looking for?

____

2 How old must applicants be?

____

3 Which club is Mark a member of?

____

4 What's he planning to study at university?

____

5 Where's he working at the moment?

____

Writing A formal letter

Student's Book page 52

6 **Where do we write these things in a formal letter? Write the numbers in the correct place on the letter.**

1 the name of the sender
2 the address of the sender
3 'Dear Sir or Madam'
4 the date
5 'Yours faithfully'
6 the address of the person who will receive the letter

> ☐ xxxxxxxxxxxxxx
> xxxxxxxxxxxxxxxx
> ☐ xxxxxxxxxx
>
> ☐ xxxxxxxxxxxx
> xxxxxxxxxxxxxx
>
> ☐ xxxxxxxxxxxxxx
>
> xxxxxxxxxxxxxxxxxxxxxxxxxxxxxxxxxxxxxx
> xxxxxxxxxxxxxxxxxxxxxxxxxxxxxxxxxxxxxx
> xxxxxxxxxxxxxxxxxxxxxxxxxxxxxxxxxxxxxx
>
> xxxxxxxxxxxxxxxxxxxxxxxxxxxxxxxxxxxxxx
> xxxxxxxxxxxxxxxxxxxxxxxxxxxxxxxxxxxxxx
> xxxxxxxxxxxxxxxxxxxxxxxxxxxxxxxxxxxxxx
> xxxxxx
>
> ☐ xxxxxxxxxxx
>
> ☐ xxxxxxxxxxx

7 Imagine you want to apply for this job. Make notes.

Music!

We are looking for a cashier and a shop assistant. Applicants must be over 14 and be interested in music.

Write to: Music! 24 High St, Brighton

Where did you see the advertisement?

___

Age? School? Subjects you study?

___

___

Want to study at university? Teachers say ...?

___

___

Where have you worked before?

___

Where are you working now?

___

Why change?

___

Earliest date to start?

___

8 Write a formal letter in your notebook applying for a job. Use your notes, the model text, and the writing guide.

Paragraph 1
I saw ... I'd like to apply ...

Paragraph 2
I'm ... years old
I'm a student ... I study ...
When I leave school ...

Paragraph 3
I'm interested in ...
I'll be able to ...

Paragraph 4
At the moment, I'm ...
Working in a ... will be ...
The earliest ...

LEARNING DIARY

		Yes	No
Vocabulary	I can name seven jobs.		
Grammar	I can describe things using comparative and superlative adjectives.		
	I can compare things using *not as … as*		
	I can talk about result using *so* and *such*.		
Pronunciation	I can recognise the weak vowel.		
Speaking	I know how to send something at the post office.		
Writing	I can write a short formal letter applying for a job.		